Saved by Grace

Saved by Grace

The Glory of Salvation in Ephesians 2

Richard D. Phillips

P U B L I S H I N G
P.O. BOX 817 • PHILLIPSBURG • NEW JERSEY 08865-0817

Italics within Scripture quotations indicate emphasis added.

Page design by Lakeside Design Plus

Printed in the United States of America

Library of Congress Cataloging-in-Publication Data

Phillips, Richard D. (Richard Davis), 1960–
Saved by grace : the glory of salvation in Ephesians 2 / Richard D. Phillips.
p. cm.
Includes bibliographical references and index.
ISBN 978-1-59638-127-8 (pbk.)
1. Salvation—Biblical teaching. 2. Bible. N.T. Ephesians II—Theology. 3. Bible. N.T. Ephesians II—Commentaries. I. Title.
BS2695.6.S25P485 2009
227'.5077—dc22

2008047346

To

Ellie
with all my heart

and to

Him
who is our peace

Ephesians 2:14

Contents

Preface

If there were ever a time when Christians could benefit from a careful study of the second chapter of Ephesians, that time would surely be now. Indeed, this statement could be made about nearly every other generation of the Christian church as well, for there is hardly a more vital need than for Christians of every age to understand the Bible's teaching on God's way of salvation. And as Martyn Lloyd-Jones wrote of Ephesians 2: "I know of no chapter in the Bible which states so clearly and so perfectly at one and the same time the essential evangelical message for the unbeliever and the status and the privileges of the believer."[1]

While the value of this chapter is vital for every era, it remains true that its teaching is especially needed today. It is always necessary for believers to comprehend God's sovereign grace in our salvation, and Ephesians 2 will fill our minds and hearts with wonder and joy for the great salvation that is God's gift to believers in Christ. Moreover, one thinks of the recent battles over the doctrine of justification and the remarkably widespread confusion even in Reformed churches regarding the relationship between faith and works. Ephesians 2 will answer these questions with clear apostolic instruction, teaching us that we are justified by faith alone, "not a result of works, so that no one may boast" (Eph. 2:9). Yet we are saved to good works, since Christians are "created in Christ Jesus for good works, which God prepared beforehand" (Eph. 2:10). It is worth observing how this chapter's teaching is neglected by those espousing the so-called New Perspective on Paul, since the apostle here so clearly refutes their conclusions. A careful and believing study of Ephesians 2 will restore us to the evangelical Reformed heritage of our fathers, with confidence in the Bible's teaching of justification through faith alone.

But this is by no means the only doctrinal issue to which Ephesians 2 speaks with authority. Take the perennial question of the relationship between regeneration and faith. Does faith precede the new birth? A thoughtful understanding of Paul's teaching of fallen man's sinful state will exclude such a possibility, since before the new birth man is "dead in . . . trespasses and sins" (Eph. 2:1). Paul presents our salvation as a spiritual resurrection that is the sovereign act of God's merciful grace (see Eph. 2:4–5). Another contended issue is the meaning of union with Christ. Paul clarifies that believers are made alive, raised up, and seated together with Christ (Eph. 2:5–6). And what about concerns today that the evangelical gospel does not adequately address man in his relationship with others and the world? Must we jettison an emphasis on individual salvation in order to restore a corporate awareness? Not if Ephesians 2 is consulted, for here we find that individual sinners are saved into a new humanity (Eph. 2:15), so that we are together citizens of God's kingdom, members of his household, and a holy temple in which God is pleased to dwell (Eph. 2:19–22).

These are just the most obvious doctrinal questions for which there is a need for contemporary answers; many others are also dealt with here in spiritually uplifting apostolic style. In short, Ephesians 2 is a veritable Rosetta stone for untangling the doctrinal confusion besetting us today, and a renewal of emphasis on Paul's teaching here will greatly serve the cause of gospel vitality in our lives and churches. I therefore pray that these studies in Ephesians 2 will be blessed by God to shine gospel light not only into troubled minds but also into the hearts of all who read them.

I wish to thank the session and congregation of First Presbyterian Church of Coral Springs, Florida, to whom these messages were first preached, as well as the session and congregation of Second Presbyterian Church of Greenville, South Carolina, for their loving prayer and support of my writing and speaking ministry. I especially thank my dear wife, Sharon, who is such an indispensable help to my ministry and joy to my heart, as well as our five children, who bear with their father in his service to Christ. This book is dedicated to my dearly beloved daughter and sister in Christ, Ellie, and to our dear Lord Jesus, who is my peace.

Richard D. Phillips
Greenville, South Carolina
Summer 2008

1

Dead in Sin

Ephesians 2:1–3

And you were dead in the trespasses and sins in which you once walked, following the course of this world, following the prince of the power of the air, the spirit that is now at work in the sons of disobedience—among whom we all once lived in the passions of our flesh, carrying out the desires of the body and the mind, and were by nature children of wrath, like the rest of mankind.
—Ephesians 2:1–3

The apostle Paul first came to Ephesus toward the end of his second missionary journey. Having traversed the northern part of today's western Turkey, he caught ship for the Macedonian city of Philippi. After bringing the gospel to Philippi, Paul moved southward through Greece, on an epic evangelizing mission that founded the churches in Thessalonica, Berea, Athens, and Corinth. One result of this itinerary was that Paul bypassed the great and cosmopolitan city of Ephesus, the regional center of the Roman province of Asia (western Turkey).

For this reason, the first notable evangelist in Ephesus was not Paul, but the eloquent Alexandrian, Apollos. It is hard to say who started the Ephesian church because when Apollos began his preaching there, disciples such as Priscilla and Aquila, who were fleeing from the first Roman persecution of Christians, were already there. Apollos was bold and persuasive as he preached in the synagogues of Ephesus. But his grasp of the gospel was incomplete. Luke records that "he knew only the baptism of John" (Acts 18:25), which suggests an unbalanced emphasis on repentance from sin over faith in the finished work of Christ. Priscilla and Aquila helped Apollos to understand the gospel more accurately, and arranged for him to cross over to Greece, to help the believers there in their apologetic struggle with the anti-Christian Jews (Acts 18:26–28).

Apollos's arrival in Greece coincided with Paul's departure from Greece for Ephesus. Apparently unaware of Apollos's ministry, Paul met professing Christian believers. He asked them, "Did you receive the Holy Spirit when you believed?" (Acts 19:2). This referred to the Pentecostal experience that occurred whenever the apostolic gospel first penetrated a new people. When the Ephesians replied that they had not received the Holy Spirit, Paul picked up the gospel where Apollos had left off, moving forward from John the Baptist's call to prepare for the coming of God's kingdom to the arrival of the kingdom of God in the life, death, and resurrection of Jesus Christ. When the Ephesians believed, Paul baptized them in the name of Christ. Then "the Holy Spirit came on them, and they began speaking in tongues and prophesying" (Acts 19:6).

Thus, from the very start of Paul's ministry in Ephesus, the apostle was concerned for the accuracy of the gospel message of salvation. Remaining in that strategic center for two years, Paul devoted himself not so much to Jewish apologetics, but to the sound instruction of the church in the doctrines of the gospel and the evangelizing of the city through the preaching of God's Word. From his pulpit in the hall of Tyrannus, Paul spoke daily, "so that all the residents of Asia heard the word of the Lord, both Jews and Greeks" (Acts 19:10).

Perhaps it was because of his initial experience in Ephesus—not to mention the strategic importance of the city to the early church—that Paul's letter to the Ephesians delivers such a clear, coherent, and comprehensive exposition of the Christian doctrine of salvation. Having begun this letter, considered by many to be the crown of all Paul's writings, with a doctrinally rich hymn of praise to God's glory in chapter 1, Paul lays out the heart of his message in chapter 2: the apostolic message of salvation. Klyne Snodgrass describes this chapter as "one of the clearest, most expressive, and most loved descriptions of salvation in the New Testament."[1]

What Is Sin?

We always want to be careful to begin our understanding of biblical doctrines where the Bible itself begins. This is especially important in this chapter, in which Paul wants us first to know what we have been saved from, and what kind of people we were when God came to us with his saving grace. Paul begins:

> And you were dead in the trespasses and sins in which you once walked, following the course of this world, following the prince of the power of the air, the spirit

> that is now at work in the sons of disobedience—among whom we all once lived in the passions of our flesh, carrying out the desires of the body and the mind, and were by nature children of wrath, like the rest of mankind. (Eph. 2:1–3)

The apostle's purpose is to show us the spiritual condition of everyone apart from Christ, and especially to show that God's work of redemption begins with a recognition of our complete sinfulness.

When we begin to talk about sin, it is important that we have a biblical understanding of what sin is. Paul supplies this understanding by using two words that together summarize the Bible's teaching on sin. Paul says that we were dead in "trespasses and sins." The first of these terms, "trespasses" (Greek, *paraptōmasin*), indicates deviating from the right course, crossing a boundary, or breaking a command. This expresses our rebellion against God's rule. God has said, "You shall not," but we have. God has said, "You shall," but we have not. All of us are guilty of trespasses, for we have not kept God's law perfectly.

The second word, translated here simply as "sins" (Greek, *hamartiais*), means "falling short of the mark." It is used of an arrow that lands short of the target. It means failing to meet the required standard—in this case, God's perfect standard of holiness. In Romans 3:23, Paul says that this applies to all of us: "all have sinned and fall short of the glory of God." We are not the people that God intended us to be.

Sin Is Death

The Bible teaches that God made mankind good, without sin. Man's fall into sin is chronicled in Genesis 3. In Genesis 2:17 God forbade Adam and Eve to eat from the tree of the knowledge of good and evil, on pain of the punishment of death. When the devil tempted our first parents so that they broke this command and sinned for the first time, the curse of death fell upon our race. As Paul explains in Romans 5:12, "sin came into the world through one man, and death through sin."

This raises a vital question to which our passage gives an important answer: Just how sinful are we apart from Jesus Christ? Exactly what effect has the fall into sin had on mankind?

There have historically been three views about man in his relationship to sin. The first is the view of liberal theology, otherwise known as *humanism.* According to this view, man, despite his occasional mistakes, is *well.* People are basically good, and left to themselves under normal circumstances, they can be expected to do good things. So far as the fall was concerned, it was a fall *upward.* By experimenting with good and evil, by not allowing God's commands to hold him back, man is growing into his true divine potential.

The liberal rabbi Harold Kushner argues just this point in a recent book, stating that by breaking God's commands in the garden of Eden, Adam and Eve expanded their horizons; this, Kushner is so bold to say, is what God was hoping our first parents would do. Kushner sees sin not as causing man's expulsion from Paradise, but as "the story of the first human beings graduating" into a world of choices and liberation. "I don't believe that eating from the Tree of Knowledge was sinful," he writes, "[but] one of the bravest and most liberating events in the history of the human race."[2]

According to the Bible, however, sin produced not liberation but separation from the holy rule of God to the cursed domination of Satan, and from the blessing of God's favor to the curse and death that is the life of sin. Perhaps the greatest condemnation of Kushner and others who espouse the liberal, upward view of the fall is their agreement with the serpent, who assured Adam and Eve that by sin, "you will not surely die," but "your eyes will be opened, and you will be like God" (Gen. 3:4–5).

The second view, held by many evangelicals today, strongly contends with the liberal view by insisting that the fall was downward. But this view sees that having fallen into sin, man is merely *sick*. This is the view of *Arminianism*, so named for the sixteenth-century theologian Jacob Arminius. He insisted that while man has certainly been corrupted by sin, his fallen condition is not so bad as to render him incapable of cooperation in salvation. Often the analogy will be made of a man who is on his deathbed. He is so weak that he cannot get out of bed, so he needs the doctor to bring the medicine that will heal him. His hand may be so weak that he cannot even hold the spoon. Nonetheless, if he is going to take the medicine, he must, by his own power and will, open his mouth to receive the saving fluid. The medicine is God's grace, without which the sick man cannot possibly be healed or even escape death. But he retains some small power, and he must exercise it if he is to be saved. Thus, the exercising of his free will is the key to his salvation.

The third view is that held by Reformed theology, also associated with the great ancient theologian Aurelius Augustine, and sometimes called *Calvinism*, for the Protestant Reformer John Calvin. This view says that man in sin certainly is not well. But neither is he merely sick. His condition is far worse than this: he is, as Paul reveals in verse 1, "dead in . . . trespasses and sins." What fallen man needs is not medicine but a resurrection. His salvation depends, as Paul wrote in Romans 9:16, "not on human will or exertion, but on God, who has mercy."

This is the Bible's teaching about men and women in sin. We are not well, not even sick, but spiritually dead. Paul does not mean that we lack biological life: we still walk and talk, eat, drink, and work. But doing all this in the realm of sin, we are dead to the things of God.

We know someone is dead because he no longer responds to stimuli. We talk to him, but he does not answer. We touch him, and he does not move. This is the way in which people who are spiritually dead respond to God and his Word: they have no comprehension, even when the Bible is taught; when the gospel offer is made, they do not respond. Martyn Lloyd-Jones puts this truth in practical terms:

> The man who is not a Christian finds the Bible very boring, and expositions of the Bible very boring. He does not find films boring, he does not find the newspapers boring, he does not find the novels boring; but he finds these things boring. He does not enjoy conversations about the soul and about life and death and heaven and God and the Lord Jesus Christ. He cannot help it, but he just sees nothing in it and he is not interested. He is interested in men and their appearance, and in what they have done and in what they have said; the world and its affairs appeal to him tremendously. The position is perfectly simple; these other things are spiritual, they are God's things, and that kind of man sees nothing in them. Why? Because he is "dead" and has no spiritual life.[3]

The famous nineteenth-century philosopher and father of utilitarianism, Jeremy Bentham, provides us with an illustration. When he died, he gave his great wealth to the University College Hospital of London—on one condition. His body was to be preserved, and at every meeting of the board of directors his corpse was to be dressed in a formal suit and seated at the boardroom table. He seems to have intended in this grisly way to remind them of his views and intellectual legacy. To this day, Jeremy Bentham's body, now dead for more than 180 years, is wheeled out for board meetings. As he is brought in, the chairman says, "Jeremy Bentham, present but not voting."[4]

Bentham is there, but he can do nothing, he can contribute nothing, he can say nothing. He hears nothing that is said. Though present, he is dead. That is a vivid picture of how he lived with respect to the things of God, and what we all are like until we are brought to spiritual life by Christ's resurrection power.

"All"—"By Nature"

You may be thinking, "I can see how this applies to some people, but I doubt that it applies to most of us—and it certainly is not true of me!" But notice that Paul specifies in verse 2 that "we all" were like this. According to Paul, this is the universal condition of mankind apart from the saving grace of God. You may pass as respectable in the sight of men, but in the sight of God all have sinned, all have trespassed, and apart from Christ all are dead in sin.

In verse 3, Paul tells us why all are dead in sin: we were "by nature children of wrath," meaning that we deserve God's condemnation. But the key expression is that this is true of us *by our nature.* This is why we are all dead in trespasses: because since the fall, our whole beings are corrupted by sin. We are not sinners because we sin; we sin because we are by nature sinners.

When Adam and Eve disobeyed God, they did not immediately experience physical death, though ultimately they did die. More importantly, they died spiritually. This is shown by the fact that they ran from God in the garden and tried to cover their nakedness with fig leaves. As Augustine explained, the kind of death Adam experienced was "God's desertion of the soul."[5] He added, "The punishment for that sin . . . was, to put it in a single word, more disobedience."[6] Death entered into man's nature as moral and spiritual corruption, so that Paul could write elsewhere of sinful people, "she... is dead even while she lives" (1 Tim. 5:6).

Our problem is that this condition has been passed on to us: this is what is meant by the doctrine of *original sin.* Original sin is not the first sin itself committed by Adam and Eve. It is the consequence of that sin as it has plunged our entire race into the corruption of depravity. It means that we are now born with natures inclined to evil. John Calvin explains, "For all of us tend to evil, and we are not only inclined to it, but we are, as it were, boiling hot with it."[7]

This principle can be proved by the sinfulness of our children from the most tender age. King David said in Psalm 51:5, "Behold, I was brought forth in iniquity, and in sin did my mother conceive me." Anyone who has raised little children knows what he was talking about. J. C. Ryle, who loved children dearly, gives this realistic assessment:

> The fairest babe, that has entered life this year and become the sunbeam of a family, is not, as its mother perhaps fondly calls it, a little "angel", or a little "innocent", but a little "sinner". Alas! As it lies smiling and crowing in its cradle, that little creature carries in its heart the seeds of every kind of wickedness! Only watch it carefully, as it grows in stature and its mind develops, and . . . you will see in it the buds and germs of deceit, evil temper, selfishness, self-will, obstinacy, greediness, envy, jealousy, passion, which, if indulged and let alone, will shoot up with painful rapidity. Who taught the child these things? Where did he learn them?[8]

The answer is that he did not learn them—transgression and sin come naturally to our race without instruction. This is why training in righteousness is so hard, while children can learn the ways of sin at the first exposure. We are all "by nature children of wrath."

This is the great and universal problem of all mankind. Our problem is not mere ignorance or lack of education; America has the most educated population of all time, but we have not graduated beyond the problem of sin. Our problem is not a bad environment, however bad our situation may in fact be; being by nature spiritually dead sinners, we are the ones who ruin every good environment. Our problem is not lack of money, so that it can be fixed by winning the lottery or by advancement at work; nor is it lack of technique, so that the right self-help advice will set us all straight. Our great problem is this, as John MacArthur explains: "Because [man] is dead to God, he is dead to spiritual life, truth, righteousness, inner peace and happiness, and ultimately to every other good thing."[9] The leopard cannot change its spots, and we cannot escape our guilty and corrupt nature, and so are hopeless unless we are saved by God.

Sin Reduces Us to Cravings

Paul continues in these verses to work out the implications of this spiritual deadness. What does it mean to be dead in sin? Paul tells us, in verse 3, that *sin reduces us to cravings.* Men and women were made in the image of God, to reflect his glory and partake of his holiness. But being dead in trespasses and sins, as Paul tells his Christian readers, "we all once lived in the passions of our flesh, carrying out the desires of the body and the mind" (Eph. 2:3).

Several key words are in play here, the first of which is translated "lived" (Greek, *anestraphēmen*) and really denotes a lifestyle. Paul says that sinfulness is characterized by a certain way of life. The second key word is translated "passions" (Greek, *epithymiais*). This could also be rendered as "lusts." Man in sin lives according to the lusts of his flesh, that is, his sinful nature.

Surely this is an apt description of our culture. The American lifestyle is driven by sinful cravings. We immediately think of the sensuality that dominates our society. Almost anything can be sold with an ad featuring a scantily clad woman. The pornography industry is booming as never before; by any estimate, a significant portion of Internet commerce today is driven by the sexual lusts of men. We add to this other cravings—the lust for money, for narcotic highs, for drunken stupors—and our society demonstrates perfectly how sin reduces men and women to animal cravings.

Paul adds that we are "carrying out the desires of the body and the mind." Literally, this reads, "doing the will of the flesh and the mind." By "mind," Paul means our *thoughts*—in this case our evil thoughts. Secular people boast about their free will, and even many Christians insist that unbelievers have a free will. But Paul knows that their will is bound to their sinful nature and to their wicked thoughts. They have a will, but it is always governed by their desires. Later in Ephesians, Paul explains, "They are darkened in their understanding, alienated from the life of God because of the ignorance that is in them, due to their hardness of heart. They have become callous and have given themselves up to sensuality, greedy to practice every kind of impurity" (4:18–19). This perfectly describes the morass into which America has sunk, just like the Roman world of Paul's day.

The apostle James chronicled this downslide in James 4:1–2: "What causes quarrels and what causes fights among you?" he asks. "Is it not this, that your passions are at war within you? You desire and do not have, so you murder. You covet and cannot obtain, so you fight and quarrel." If you merely buy into the covetousness of our consumer society, and especially if you drink from the entertainment trough of sensual sin, you are a vital part of this devastating reign of death. By sin, man, alienated from God, spiritually dead and enslaved, is reduced to the level of the beast, living in misery and perpetually unsatisfied desire.

Sin Leads to Our Eternal Destruction

The last thing Paul tells us about mankind's being dead in sin is that *sin leads to our eternal destruction*: we "were by nature children of wrath, like the rest of mankind" (Eph. 2:3).

The Bible teaches clearly that God judges both sin and the sinner. People say that God hates the sin and loves the sinner. That is true, in that he offers salvation for sinners in Jesus Christ. But in the end, in the great day of God's final judgment, it will not merely be sins but sinners who are cast into the fiery chasm of hell.

God's holiness demands that his wrath be poured out on sin. He proved this at the cross, for even when it was his own perfect Son who bore our sins, God poured out the full furies of hell upon his soul. What will it be like, then, for those who bear their own sins into God's judgment, not having them forgiven through the blood of Jesus Christ? Paul says elsewhere that in his return as Judge, Jesus will come "in flaming fire, inflicting vengeance on those who do not know God and on those who do not obey the gospel of our Lord Jesus. They will suffer the punishment of eternal destruction, away from the presence of the Lord and from the glory of his might" (2 Thess. 1:8–9).

J. I. Packer explains, "God's wrath in the Bible is never the capricious, self-indulgent, irritable, morally ignoble thing that human anger so often is. It is, instead, a right and necessary reaction to objective moral evil."[10] Therefore, to be dead in sins is ultimately to suffer eternal death—not annihilation, but eternal condemnation and judgment in the wrathful hands of a holy God.

Jesus Christ Is the Solution to Sin

I have learned as a preacher that people do not like to hear about sin. Not much, anyway. But according to Paul, if we ignore or avoid the subject, we cannot understand the salvation that God offers us in Christ. Paul shows us that the only way to understand and receive salvation is to admit and confess our sin. The point of talking about sin is not to tear people down, but to enter them onto God's saving path at his appointed place of entry. The Bible says, "Humble yourselves in the sight of the Lord, and He will lift you up" (James 4:10 NKJV).

I can imagine going into a leper colony to preach, to find that people there don't like to hear about leprosy all the time, or to preach to blind people who don't want to always talk about blindness. Along those lines, I understand why sinners don't want to hear about sin; they have to deal with it enough and could use something cheerier.

But what if you went into the leper colony having the cure to their disease? Wouldn't it, then, be your duty to talk about it? So it is with sin in the church and in the Bible. It may seem good to have your mind relieved from the pain and anxiety of sin with some pulpit comedy or sentimental stories. But it is decisively better to have your sin conquered, overcome, and removed. That is why the Bible constantly talks about sin, why our worship must always bring us as sinners to the cross of Christ, and why faithful preaching does not shrink from pointing us to the problem of sin. You may go elsewhere to be entertained or to find an emotional lift.

But the church of Jesus Christ is about salvation, and salvation requires that we face the facts about sin.

Sin is the great problem of the world, for which man has no solution. But here is good news; here is the light that has dawned in the land of the shadow of death. Jesus Christ has conquered sin by dying on the cross as an offering for us, and he offers salvation to all who will come, confess their need, and believe on him. He offers life to the dead, freedom for those in bondage, and heaven for those bound for hell.

This is something not only for non-Christians but for believers in Christ to hear and remember. It was to Christians that Paul wrote this epistle. Christians need to hear about sin as a means of recalling the wonder of what God has done in our salvation and to make alive our love to God. If we want to realize the greatness of the salvation that God has given us by his grace, then we must realize the depths to which we had sunk and the helplessness from which he saved us in Christ. We preach sin not to beat people down, but as the first step to lifting them up with the saving grace of God.

The glory of Christianity is that we can not only feel better for a while, but be made better forever. Not only can we experience holy religious moments, but we can be holy in Christ. Not only can we escape for a time the thoughts about ours and others' sins and the pain of a dying, sinful, cursed world, but we can be cleansed of sin and made a part of the new and sinless resurrection world. We can be forgiven, be born again, and enter a new life; not one that is governed by sinful cravings but by a holy passion for God—a life that leads not to eternal destruction in shame but to everlasting life in glory.

How does this happen? It happens by coming as sinners to the Savior, Jesus Christ. First, this means confessing that you have been dead in trespasses, you have been reduced to cravings and to the bondage of a corrupt soul, and you have been worthy of eternal condemnation in the court of God's justice. Then it means trusting Jesus to take your sins away by his death on the cross in your place, and then to send the Holy Spirit to make you spiritually alive forever.

"The wages of sin is death," Paul wrote in Romans 6:23, "but the free gift of God is eternal life in Christ Jesus our Lord." Sin is bondage to lusts and cravings. But Jesus said, "If you abide in my word, . . . you will know the truth, and the truth will set you free" (John 8:31–32). Sin leads to eternal destruction and damnation, but Jesus said, "I am the resurrection and the life. Whoever believes in me, though he die, yet shall he live" (John 11:25–26). "Truly, truly," Jesus said, "whoever hears my word and believes him who sent me has eternal life. He does not come into judgment, but has passed from death to life" (John 5:24).

From death to life. From bondage to holy liberty. From wrath to resurrection. Believe on the Lord Jesus Christ, and you will be saved.

Questions for Study and Reflection

1. Why is it so important to our understanding of the gospel for us to understand the biblical doctrine of sin? Why do some people resent this topic?
2. Just how sinful are we apart from Jesus Christ? What are the effects of Adam's fall into sin upon us today?
3. What are three possibilities for understanding the Fall? Which is the biblical teaching?
4. What is meant by "original sin"? How does original sin affect us today?
5. How does Jesus change the bad news of sin into good news of salvation? How would you explain Christ's remedy for sin to a friend?

2

The World, the Devil, and the Flesh

Ephesians 2:1–3

And you were dead in the trespasses and sins in which you once walked, following the course of this world, following the prince of the power of the air, the spirit that is now at work in the sons of disobedience—among whom we all once lived in the passions of our flesh, carrying out the desires of the body and the mind, and were by nature children of wrath, like the rest of mankind.
—Ephesians 2:1–3

In the opening words of Ephesians 2, the apostle Paul describes man apart from Christ as "dead in . . . trespasses and sins." It may seem surprising that having described us this way, he then goes on to talk about the way in which we lived. We lived but were dead; we were dead but we lived. This is the second major point he makes about life in sin in these opening verses of Ephesians 2. Paul wants us to know that in sin man is spiritually dead. But he also wants us to know what kind of life it is that spiritually dead sinners live.

Paul gives us here as profound and accurate a description of the life in sin that you will find anywhere in the Bible. His purpose is no doubt in part to show us the ugly truth so that we will not be tempted to return to this life of bondage. More importantly, he wants believers to know how great is the obstacle that sin posed to our fellowship with God, thus how great is the salvation that God has given us in Christ, and then how great is the power that is available to us who once lived this way but now live in the strength of God's Holy Spirit.

Paul obviously considers it important for us to understand what sin is all about. The reason is that apart from an understanding of sin, we cannot understand Christianity as a whole. Take the doctrine of the incarnation. Why did the eternal Son of God have to take up flesh and live in this world? Because of the greatness of the problem of sin. Because man, whom God created for himself, was spiritually dead and in bondage to sin. People who say that they don't want to talk about sin therefore don't want to know the purpose for Christ's coming into the world. This is what the angel said to Joseph before Jesus was born: "You shall call his name Jesus, for he will save his people from their sins" (Matt. 1:21).

Take also the crucifixion of our Lord. What was it for? Peter tells us, "Christ also suffered once for sins, the righteous for the unrighteous, that he might bring us to God" (1 Peter 3:18). Furthermore, take Christ's present work in heaven. Jesus is interceding for us with the Father in heaven. Why? To deal with our present sins. John writes, "If anyone does sin, we have an advocate with the Father, Jesus Christ the righteous"

(1 John 2:1). If we are unwilling to learn about sin, then we will be unable to glorify the Lord Jesus as we should. It is the greatness of our sin, which he totally overcomes, that measures the greatness of his love for us.

Not only can you not understand Jesus Christ and Christianity, but unless you face the biblical facts regarding sin, you cannot understand the world as it is. Martyn Lloyd-Jones writes:

> You cannot understand the whole of human history apart from this, with all its wars and its quarrels and its conquests, its calamities, and all that it records. I assert that there is no adequate explanation save in the biblical doctrine of sin. The history of the world can only be understood truly in the light of this great biblical doctrine of man, fallen and in sin.[1]

Finally, unless you understand the Bible's doctrine of sin, you cannot even understand yourself. Sin is the power that has been and wants to keep controlling your life, and from which you must be delivered by the saving reign of Christ.

Therefore, let us be willing, as Christians, to look into the matter of sin.

In the last chapter, we saw the results of sin: sin is death, sin reduces us to cravings, and sin leads to eternal destruction. Now we will look back over these verses to see Paul's teaching on what the life in sin is like. He tells us that life in sin is bondage to three great powers: the world, the devil, and the flesh. These we need to understand and be delivered from by the redeeming work of Jesus Christ.

Following the Course of This World

What does it mean to live in sin? First, Paul tells us that it is *to live in conformity with the world.* He writes, "You were dead in the trespasses and sins in which you once walked, following the course of this world" (vv. 1–2).

The Bible uses the term "world" in a variety of ways. John 3:16 says that "God so loved the world that He gave His only begotten Son" (NKJV). In that case, "world" speaks of the human race in its entirety. More often, however, "world" speaks of the world system that is in rebellion against God. In Galatians 1:4, Paul refers to it as "the present evil age." The antithesis between God and the world is best stated in 1 John 2:15–16: "Do not love the world or the things in the world. If anyone loves the world, the love of the Father is not in him. For all that is in the world—the desires of the flesh and the desires of the eyes and pride in possessions—is not from the Father but is from the world."

This is what Paul has in mind when he is speaking about living in conformity with the world. He means the world in its values, in its materialism, in its unbelief and opposition to the rule of God. Leon Morris observes that Paul "reminds the Ephesians that before they became Christians they not only were dead in their sinfulness, but their pattern of life was one dictated by the world in which they lived and not by any such motive as a pure desire to do the will of God. . . . The world is always sensual and obviously given over to evil."[2]

Much of Paul's desire is for his readers not to walk in the ways of the world, but rather to walk in good works (Eph. 2:10), to walk worthily of their calling (4:1), to "walk in love" (5:2), and to "walk as children of light" (5:8). By speaking of a walk, Paul means our active approach to life, which should not be worldly but godly. As he famously put it in Romans 12:2, "Do not be conformed to this world, but be transformed by the renewal of your mind."

Paul's statement in verse 2 is that non-Christian people, those who are dead in sin, are controlled by the world. They are "following the course of this world." There is nothing easier to prove than this. The world demands conformity and will ostracize and ridicule you if you do not conform. We learn this from an early age, and the result is that people's ideas are derived from the newspapers, television, and Internet. The way people dress, how they talk, their hairstyles, and the music they listen to are utterly controlled by the latest fashion that is praised in the media and thus by other people.

Undoubtedly, the most powerful influence of our time is television. It is nothing less than astonishing to see how in a few generations, television has almost eradicated the Christian values that once formed the backbone of our nation and replaced them with other values once utterly rejected as pagan. How did this happen? Not by presenting fair and rational arguments, but by making sin seem attractive and pleasurable; living in a godly manner is not so much repudiated intellectually but made to seem narrow and stupid and lame. For this reason the amount of television you watch is at least related to how worldly you are. It is not that television and movies are inherently evil; godly themes can also be conveyed by these mediums. But it is a thoughtless imbibing of unbelieving worldviews through shows and movies that leads so many in "the course of this world."

It is hard to overestimate today how important it is for Christians not to live according to the values of the world around us. You used to hear about a category of people called "carnal Christians." This phrase designated people who were saved but who lived in accordance with the world. I am glad not to hear that expression much anymore because it is utterly unbiblical. A professing Christian who lives in a worldly manner is nothing more than a false professor of faith. In 1 Corinthians 6:9–10, Paul explains, "Do not be deceived: neither the sexually immoral, nor idolaters, nor adulterers, nor men who practice homosexuality, nor thieves, nor the greedy, nor drunkards, nor revilers, nor swindlers will inherit the kingdom of God."

What we expose ourselves to matters. Worldliness happens subtly, surreptitiously. If you want to be worldly, then just watch a lot of television, just read all the best-sellers without discrimination, just go to movies that glorify adultery and enter into the entertainment of lust and violence. Put on headphones and groove to music that rejoices in violence and hate and even glorifies death. You will become worldly all too quickly.

This applies especially to young people. They are under so much pressure to be "cool," which is often just another way of saying "worldly." Therefore, young Christians must be helped to understand that to follow Christ is to take up the cross. Either we can follow "the course of this world" or we can follow Jesus Christ. Either we can be followers of Christ along his narrow way that leads to life or we can join the broad way that leads to death (cf. Luke 13:24). The apostle John warns us, "The world is passing away along with its desires, but whoever does the will of God abides forever" (1 John 2:17).

If this is true of Christian individuals, surely the worst thing the church can do is to pattern itself after the world. Yet churches are usually criticized today for being not too worldly but too holy. It is a mortal sin of the church growth movement to make anyone uncomfortable in the church. But to be used by God, to make a difference for Christ in our time, we must be willing to be different—not because we are trying to be stuffy or formal or high and mighty, but because we are trying to be biblical. When we do this, the world notices that there is something different about us. Many will scoff, but others will come in and pay attention and be saved. Lloyd-Jones summarizes this well:

> The glory of the gospel is that when the Church is absolutely different from the world, she invariably attracts it. It is then that the world is made to listen to her mes-

> sage, though it may hate it at first. . . . It should not be our ambition to be as much like everybody else as we can, though we happen to be Christian, but . . . our ambition should be to be like Christ, the more like Him the better, and the more like Him we become, the more we shall be unlike everybody who is not a Christian.[3]

Following the Prince of the Power of the Air

The first power governing people in sin is the world. Second, Paul directs our attention to a power that is much more sinister. To live in sin, he says, is *to live under the domination of the devil.* He says that the man or woman in sin follows "the prince of the power of the air, the spirit that is now at work in the sons of disobedience" (v. 2).

This term may sound like a strange designation for the devil, but it is consistent with his portrayal all through the Bible. By "air" Paul means the spirit realm. The devil, or Satan, is the ruler of the evil spiritual powers, and his rebellious spirit energizes all the disobedience of mankind. In Ephesians 6:12, Paul writes, "For we do not wrestle against flesh and blood, but against the rulers, against the authorities, against the cosmic powers over this present darkness, against the spiritual forces of evil in the heavenly places." Jesus called Satan, in John 12:31, "the ruler of this world," and in 2 Corinthians 4:4, Paul called him "the god of this world," who blinds the minds of unbelievers.

Satan is not, in fact, a god, but rather a fallen archangel. Yet he has usurped the place of God in the lives of men and women in sin. Augustine said that man is like a horse and can have only one of two riders. Either the horse is ridden by God or it is ridden by Satan. Paul teaches here that those who are dead to God are under Satan's rule; indeed, they are realizing the devil's fondest ambitions by rebelling against God and destroying themselves in sin.

Furthermore, Paul tells us how this works. He says that Satan is "the spirit that is now at work in the sons of disobedience." The verb translated "at work" is the Greek word *energeō*, from which we get the noun *energy* and the verb *energize.* Paul used this same verb in Ephesians 1:19–20, when he reminded the Christians about the "greatness of [God's] power toward us who believe, according to the working [that is, energizing] of his great might that he worked [energized] in Christ when he raised him from the dead." It is God by his Holy Spirit who energizes godliness, just as he energized Christ's resurrection, and it is the devil who by his evil spirit energizes all disobedience. Satan is the spirit of the age—this present evil, condemned world in which we live.

It was the devil's influence that caused our first parents to plunge our race into the corruption of sin. He is still at work, and his aim is always the same as it was at first—to insinuate that God is not really good and that his ways will hold us back, to tempt us to believe that through sin we will find fulfillment. When we sin, he then accuses us so that we believe that God will never take us back. The devil rules a vast host of demons who operate unseen, carrying out his program of rebellion and sin.

Most significant to Paul's thought here is not the temptation that the devil or his minions might directly inflict on us. Rather, it is that as the ruler of this world, he controls the world and supplies it with its evil values. Surely you do not think it is by chance that a culture that turns from God always takes on the same characteristics! It is not by chance that a godless people become sensual and violent, that families break down and moral absolutes are discarded, that poverty and ignorance and cruelty begin to reign. This is the rule of Satan, and it happens wherever God's rule is denied, either individually or on a grand scale.

If you wonder why the world's entertainment leaders keep pushing further and further into sin, this is why. If you wonder why the legislatures and the courts advance into pagan ways of thinking, this is why. There is a spirit to the age, and Satan is energizing the rebellion of the world. This is why the fashion leaders and the best sellers and the trendsetters all seem to be taking us in the same direction. James Montgomery Boice comments, "This tells how the devil enslaves men and women. It is not that he is personally present. He is only one creature and can only be present in one place at one time. It is rather through the evil spirit or outlook present in the world that he rules us."[4] We may be from time to time under assault from unseen spiritual powers, although most of us have probably never directly encountered the devil himself. But we are under his control when we give ourselves to sin and follow the values that are popular in the world.

Following the Will of the Flesh

Man in sin is governed by the hostile powers of the world, which affect him from without, and also by the devil, who dominates him from beyond. But there is a third force that drives everyone who lives in sin, and this is the sinful nature, or the flesh, which rules us from within. To live in sin, Paul says, is *to be dominated by the lusts of the flesh.*

We discussed this idea in the previous chapter, where I noted that sin reduces us to cravings. If we are to do the will of God, then we must gain self-control over these sinful passions, with the help of prayer and through the transforming power of God's Word. This is not something that will happen passively in our lives; it is something that we must be determined about in the power of the Holy Spirit.

If you peruse Paul's letters, you will see how deadly serious he is about the matter of not living in the lusts of our sinful nature. He writes in Romans 6:12–14: "Let not sin therefore reign in your mortal body, to make you obey its passions. Do not present your members to sin as instruments for unrighteousness, but present yourselves to God as those who have been brought from death to life, and your members to God as instruments for righteousness. For sin will have no dominion over you, since you are not under law but under grace." In Romans 13:13–14, Paul adds, "Let us walk properly as in the daytime, not in orgies and drunkenness, not in sexual immorality and sensuality, not in quarreling and jealousy. But put on the Lord Jesus Christ, and make no provision for the flesh, to gratify its desires."

The way to conquer the bondage of lusts, Paul says, is twofold. First, we must "make no provision for the flesh." This means that we are not to subject ourselves to likely sources of temptation. In our day, we think first of all about sexual morality; it is essential that Christians stand apart at this point. But different people are susceptible to different temptations. Paul lists these in Galatians 5:19–21: "Now the works of the flesh are evident: sexual immorality, impurity, sensuality, idolatry, sorcery, enmity, strife, jealousy, fits of anger, rivalries, dissensions, divisions, envy, drunkenness, orgies, and things like these. I warn you, as I warned you before, that those who do such things will not inherit the kingdom of God." In whatever ways we find ourselves driven by our sinful nature, we must come to God for forgiveness, for power in the Holy Spirit, and then apply ourselves diligently to the task of self-control.

But it is not enough merely to strive against sin and avoid temptation. We must also, as Paul said, "put on the Lord Jesus Christ" (Rom. 13:14). In the long run, the only way to avoid being enslaved by sinful desires is to become more and more like Christ, through the power of his Holy Spirit. Paul's approach to this transformation involves not merely putting off sin but also putting on the holiness of Jesus Christ: "You . . . were taught in him, as the truth is in Jesus, to put off your old self, which belongs to your former manner of life and is corrupt through deceitful desires, and to be renewed in the spirit of your minds, and to put on the new self, created after the likeness of God in true righteousness and holiness" (Eph. 4:21–24).

One of the great tragedies of the nineteenth century was that of Oscar Wilde. His brilliant mind won him the highest academic honors. His literary genius won him accolades; his charm and kindness made him well liked. But because he succumbed to fleshly temptation of various kinds, the most famous of which was homosexuality, Wilde fell from his high perch, ending up in prison and disgrace. He wrote of all this:

> The gods had given me almost everything. But I let myself be lured into long spells of senseless and sensual ease. . . . Tired of being on the heights I deliberately went to the depths in search of new sensation. . . . I grew careless of the lives of others. I took pleasure where it pleased me, and passed on. I forgot that every little action of the common day makes or unmakes character, and that therefore what one has done in the secret chamber, one has some day to cry aloud from the house-top. I allowed pleasure to dominate me. I ended in horrible disgrace.[5]

This is something for all of us to remember. When we dabble in sin, we are risking our character and the domination of the devil, who rules through the sinful passions. Sin always takes us further than we wanted to go, keeps us longer than we wanted to stay, and makes us pay far more than we ever wanted to pay—even the price of our souls.

The Banquet of the Devil and the Feast of the Lord

Life in sin is life under the domination of the devil. It is a life spent following the course of the world, the spirit of which is controlled by Satan. It is a life spent being driven by fleshly desires, which are the devil's whips to keep his slaves in line.

Therefore, the choice between righteousness and sin is nothing less than the choice between the rule of God—the holy, good, and loving Creator and Redeemer—and the rule of Satan—the lying, enslaving, accusing, destroying devil.

In a typically brilliant sermon, Charles Spurgeon depicts this choice as the choice between two banquet halls. There is the banquet of the devil and the feast of the Lord. Spurgeon takes as his theme verse a statement made at the wedding at Cana, where Jesus turned the water into wine. The wine that Jesus had miraculously made was presented to the master of the banquet, who exclaimed, "Everyone serves the good wine first, and when people have drunk freely, then the poor wine. But you have kept the good wine until now" (John 2:10).

Spurgeon explains that this is the difference between the world, the devil, and the flesh on the one hand and the Lord Jesus Christ on the other. The devil's banquet gives all its luscious pleasures up front, and only afterward do things turn sour. Spurgeon considers the experience of the man of fleshly desire, to whom the devil first comes with the sparkling cup of pleasure. It intoxicates his senses, be it sexual pleasure or narcotic pleasure or gambling or any other fleshly pleasure. He thinks, "What a fool I was, not to have tasted this before!" Spurgeon explains, "He drinks again; this time he takes a deeper draught, and the wine is hot in his veins. Oh! How blest is he! What would he not say now in the praise of Bacchus or Venus, or whatever shape Beelzebub chooses to assume? He becomes a very orator in praise of sin."[6]

But in time the first course is over, and the devil brings out a different cup. This is not the cup of pleasure but of satiation. This is the poor wine that follows the good. It lacks the excitement that the now-dulled senses crave, but gives just enough to keep him drinking. It gives only disappointment to go along with addiction.

This second cup is followed by a third, the cup of wrath and damnation. "'Drink of that,' says the devil, and the man sips it and starts back and shrieks, 'O God! that ever I must come to this!' 'You must drink, sir!' the devil replies . . . 'Drink, though it be like fire down your throat! . . . He who rebels against the laws of God, must reap the harvest.'"[7] This is the grim cup that never features in the advertisements of sin. The devil always sets forth the best wine, the pleasurable wine, first—knowing that thereby he will put the cup of wrath to the lips of our souls.

Spurgeon calls that the table of fleshly lusts in the devil's banquet hall. He also notices the table of worldliness there, and the same pattern appears. First comes the cup of riches and advancement, which brings ease and the praise of men. But the second cup comes, and it is the unexpected drink of worldly cares that weigh down the worldly man's heart. Third comes the cup of a bitter and avaricious character, so that even what a rich man has provides him no pleasure. Finally comes the same cup of wrath as before. "Drink! Drink! Drink!" says the devil as he serves his banquet: first the good wine, then the foul, and finally the poisoned cup of wrath and condemnation.

How different is the feast of the Lord Jesus Christ! His practice is exactly opposite from that of the devil. The master of the wedding said to him: "Everyone serves the good wine first, and when people have drunk freely, then the poor wine. But you have kept the good wine until now" (John 2:10).

At Jesus' table, the feast of salvation, the bitter and difficult things come first, and to those who press on in faith there are better things to come. In this life, Christ's people are often afflicted. Spurgeon writes, "Jesus brings in the cup of poverty and affliction, and makes his own children drink of it. . . . This is the way Christ begins. The worst wine is first." The same is true spiritually as with our outward circumstances. Spiritually, we must first drink the bitter cup of conviction of sin; this is the course Paul is serving in these opening verses of Ephesians chapter 2. He knew it well, having tasted it himself.

But then comes another cup. In it Jesus has mixed something better. Spurgeon writes, "I have drank of [the cup of conviction] and I thought that Jesus was unkind, but, in a little while, he brought me forth a sweeter cup, the cup of his forgiving love, filled with the rich crimson of his precious blood."[8] Jesus' second cup brings us consolation for all our trials and relief for our sense of guilt. As he drinks deeper and deeper from that cup of fellowship and love, the believer grows in communion with God, until at last he cries, "The LORD is my chosen portion and my cup. . . . The lines have fallen for me in pleasant places" (Ps. 16:5–6). Finally, Jesus brings the best cup last, the taste of which is incomprehensible in blessing to those of us still living who have yet to finally drink it. It is the cup of glory, the cup of resurrection life, the cup that makes us sing: "You make known to me the path of life; in your presence there is fullness of joy; at your right hand are pleasures forevermore" (Ps. 16:11).

This is the promise of God for all who were dead in sin, following the course of the world, obeying the prince of the power of the air, and doing the will of the flesh, but who by faith in Christ are born again to a new life, are forgiven and cleansed from all their sins, and take their place at his banquet feast. All the others serve the good wine first, but then when the people are drunk, in comes the bad. But Jesus, though he calls us now to join him at the cross, to the bitterness of facing and confessing our sins, and to the struggle of withstanding the world, the devil, and the flesh, he leads us on to the crown of life, when only the best wine will be served and where joy abounds forever. Believe on the Lord Jesus Christ, and you will be saved!

Questions for Study and Reflection

1. How does Paul's teaching on sin enable us to understand biblical doctrines such as the incarnation and crucifixion of Christ? How does it help us to understand the world, and even ourselves?
2. When Paul says that sinners have walked in "the course of this world," what does he mean by "world"? Can you cite contemporary examples of how people are controlled by the "world" today?
3. What do most people today believe about the devil? What does the Bible say about him? In what sense does Satan rule our current age? What does it mean that Satan "energizes" sin?
4. Is it of great importance for Christians to subdue the sinful cravings of their "flesh"? What means does God provide for us to do this? What is your experience in struggling against sin? Is it possible for Christians to gain power against sin? If so, how?
5. If you could give advice about sin to a new convert, what would it be?

3

But God

Ephesians 2:4

But God . . .
—Ephesians 2:4

A number of years ago, a society for the spread of atheism published a tract exposing the depravity of many great Bible heroes. One after another, the leaflet shows the villainy of such men as Abraham, Jacob, Moses, and David. Under the face of Abraham an inscription reads that here was a coward who was willing to sacrifice the honor of his wife to save his own skin. It lists the passage where Bible the Bible admits this fact and then where the Bible calls him "the friend of God." "What kind of God," it asks, "would befriend so dishonorable a man?" Under Jacob's picture is the Bible's description of Jacob as a liar and a cheat, and also where God makes him the prince of his people. What does this say about the character of a God who would call himself "the God of Jacob"? Next came the society's reminder that Moses was a murderer, yet God picked Moses to bring his law into the world. David was worst of all. He seduced Bathsheba and then had her husband killed to cover it up. Yet this is "the man after God's own heart," the leaflet complains. What kind of God could find so much to praise in a man like this, it asks, and why would anyone serve him?

How do we, as worshipers of the Bible's God, answer these questions? The first thing I would say is that everything the atheist tract says is true. It is not only true—it is a glorious truth!—that the heroes of the Bible, excepting Jesus Christ, are all scoundrels and criminals, breakers of God's law, and sinners to the core. This, by the way, shows the Bible's honesty; no other religious tome dares to display the human weakness and sins of its heroes the way the Bible does, because the Bible is not trusting in man but in God.

Furthermore, it is true that God saves people like this, making them his own friends and children and servants. God "justifies the ungodly," Paul writes (Rom. 4:5). So we agree with the atheists on this point. The difference is that we see this truth as God's glory and not his shame. Since we are sinners like the people in the Bible, the fact that God saves sinners commends him for our affection instead of subjecting him to our disdain.

This glorious truth that God saves us, in and despite our sin and shame, is the same truth that Paul teaches in the two words that begin Ephesians 2:4. In the first three verses of Ephesians 2, Paul has labored to show us the truth of what the world and the atheists say about us: that we are no better than anybody else, but in fact are far worse than even they would imagine—that we were spiritually dead, captives to the world, the devil, and the flesh, justly under the condemnation of God. Paul admits this—insists on this—and then writes two words that change everything: "But God." Martyn Lloyd-Jones comments, "These two words, in and of themselves, in a sense contain the whole of the gospel. The gospel tells of what God has done, God's intervention; it is something that comes entirely from outside us and displays to us that wondrous and astonishing work of God."[1]

These two words declare that when man's resources and strength are gone, while sin has brought us into a hopeless situation, there is yet a great hope because God himself has intervened to save us. Before God's grace we were lifeless, enslaved, and bound for condemnation. But because of what God has done in Jesus Christ, believers are made alive with Christ and raised with him to reign forever.

I want to consider these two words, "But God," in terms of what they have to say about *the Christian message,* about *the Christian's God,* and about *the Christian life.*

The Christian Message

Sometimes, in order to understand a message correctly, you must first be clear about what it does not say. I think that is a helpful exercise when it comes to Paul's presentation of the gospel in this chapter. We especially need to note that Paul is not calling us to take action. This may seem surprising, given all he has said about the terrible reality of sin. We might expect him now to say, "Let's all take a firm stand against sin. Let's organize ourselves and straighten out our lives so that we will no longer be dead in sin."

He does not say this because of what death means. Paul does say, "You were dead . . . in trespasses and sins" (Eph. 2:1), and this means that for our part the struggle is over. We are like Jesus' friend Lazarus in John chapter 11. He was dead and buried, and the one thing Jesus did not do was to wait for Lazarus to do something. Likewise, the Christian message to the world is not one of morality or spiritual exercises, or any other kind of human activity. Christianity does not offer you self-help techniques that promise to fix your life. It does not offer you stairs that you can ascend to God. Instead, Christianity tells the hard truth that in sin you are already dead, you are under God's wrath, and there is no hope in anything you can do.

Realizing this hard truth helps us understand just what the Christian gospel is. Paul writes that God has intervened at the point of our hopelessness in order to save us. This is the proclamation to which he has been moving since he began this chapter. He began, "You were dead in . . . trespasses and sins," and then he had to explain that statement: we were in slavery to the world, the devil, and the flesh, and we were objects of God's wrath. Now, in verses 4 and 5, he arrives at the solution: "But God, . . . even when we were dead in our trespasses, made us alive together with Christ." We were dead, but God has made us alive in Christ. As Jonah said in his prayer from the depths, "Salvation is of the LORD" (Jonah 2:9 NKJV).

The atheists complain about the sins of Abraham and Jacob, Moses and David. But perhaps the best example of sin and salvation comes from even earlier in the Bible. Adam and Eve were placed in the garden of Eden with every blessing they could possibly hope for. God merely insisted that they acknowledge him as Lord, forbidding them to eat from the tree of the knowledge of good and evil (Gen. 2:16–17). Not eating from this tree symbolized their willingness to rely on God and do his will in all things, not to be their own gods, deciding right and wrong for themselves. But tempted by the devil, our first parents disobeyed that one prohibition and fell into sin. Lloyd-Jones asks:

> What defence is there for Adam and Eve, made in the image of God, in Paradise, in absolute perfec-

> tion with the friendship and the companionship of God, with all the blessings that anybody could ever desire? What did they do? They deliberately rebelled against God; they disobeyed him and put their own wills before his. Is there any excuse for them? Can any plea be put forward?[2]

Adam and Eve had no excuse. They could not plead ignorance, for God had clearly revealed his will. They could not say they hadn't been warned, because they had. "Nothing can be said for them. They had no defence and deserved not only to be driven out of Paradise, but to be destroyed totally and eternally."[3]

The same is true of us. We have no excuse for our sin. We cannot plead ignorance of God's law, which has been taught in the Bible and is stamped by God on our consciences. We have deliberately flouted our knowledge of right and wrong. God has created us, has given us everything good, has told us clearly of our obligation before him, and has warned us of the penalty of death that resides in sin. Lloyd-Jones therefore concludes: "We must realize that as members of the human race we deserve nothing but total destruction."[4] We may blame God, as so many do, but the fact is that we ourselves are at fault.

Let's return to Adam and Eve. They had sinned and were under God's judgment. They were guilty and at fault. What now could they do? First, they tried to evade God's wrath, putting on fig leaves and running away. These are still our main strategies: to cover our sin with the false righteousness of supposedly good works, corrupted as they are by sin, or to seek to forget or deny the reality of God. Adam and Eve failed to escape because God is God; he saw them and he found them out. As the psalmist says, "Where shall I go from your Spirit? Or where shall I flee from your presence? If I ascend to heaven, you are there! If I make my bed in Sheol, you are there!" (Ps. 139:7–8). Then our first parents tried to blame God, but God knows all things and cannot be fooled. God is the Judge, and he is not threatened by our petty complaints and accusations.

You see their predicament. When God came to Adam and Eve, they could do nothing to make themselves right with God. They could not remove their guilt. They could not erase their responsibility. They could not deny the corruption of sin in their hearts or keep sin from tainting any good works they might offer to assuage God's wrath.

So what happened to our first parents? Were they eternally destroyed, as they might well have been? The answer is found in Paul's statement: "But God." Genesis 3:21 tells us what God did to save them, because for all their sin and guilt God loved them still: "The LORD God made for Adam and for his wife garments of skins and clothed them." God was under no obligation to save Adam and Eve, but he did. He did it by sacrificing an innocent animal in their place, transferring their guilt to the substitute that bore the penalty of death for them, and then clothing them in its innocent skin. That was a picture, of course, of what God was going to do through Jesus Christ, to save all his people from their sin.

What was true of Adam and Eve is true of us all. We are hopeless in our guilt and our sin, without any way of making right all that is wrong. Isaiah wrote of us, "All we like sheep have gone astray; we have turned—every one—to his own way." So what will happen? But God! Isaiah continues, "And the LORD has laid on him the iniquity of us all" (Isa. 53:6).

These are the two greatest words in the Bible, on which we must rest for salvation: "But God." Mankind was lost in sin, you and I were lost and condemned and without hope, but God sent his own Son to be the Lamb that was slain for us. Paul writes in Romans 5:8, "But God shows his love for us in that while we were still sinners, Christ died for us." Paul says in our passage,

"You were dead in . . . trespasses and sins. . . . But God . . . made us alive together with Christ." God sent his own Son to bear our sins on the cross, dying the death that our sins deserve, and in his resurrection power giving us eternal life.

This is the Christian message, and Augustus Toplady puts its story on our lips:

Not the labors of my hands
can fulfil thy law's demands;
Could my zeal no respite know,
could my tears forever flow,
All for sin could not atone;
thou must save, and thou alone.

Is this the message that you have believed for your salvation? Have you confessed that you are dead in sin apart from God's saving grace, and that because of his mercy and love you are saved by the work of Christ alone? Can you sing the remaining words of the hymn?

Nothing in my hand I bring,
simply to thy cross I cling;
Naked, come to thee for dress;
helpless, look to thee for grace;
Foul, I to the Fountain fly;
wash me, Savior, or I die.[5]

The Christian's God

This great teaching of Paul's tells us not only about the Christian message, but also about the Christian's God. If we are to believe this message of a salvation that is wholly of him, then that tells us much about what we have to believe about God himself.

First, this shows that *God is sovereign.* This is good news because it is a sovereign God, a God who is in active control of events in the world that he made, who can intervene for our salvation. The words "But God" go right along with Paul's teaching in chapter 1 on God's sovereignty in salvation: "He chose us in [Christ] before the foundation of the world. . . . In love he predestined us for adoption as sons through Jesus Christ, according to the purpose of his will" (Eph. 1:4–5). God's sovereignty is a comfort to his people because it says that the One on whom we utterly rely is able to accomplish all his will.

Second, the gospel shows that *God is holy and just.* Verse 3 shows that sinners are "children of wrath." People don't like to hear this doctrine, but because of God's holiness we must. God told Adam that if he sinned he would die, and that is exactly what happened. We experience physical death because of God's just punishment, and we are all born spiritually dead as the consequence of Adam's first sin.

Even God's solution to the problem of our sin shows his holiness and justice. The great Puritan theologian John Owen explains:

> To see Christ . . . beloved of the Father, fear and tremble, bow and sweat, pray and die; to see him lifted up on the cross, the earth trembling beneath him as if unable to bear his weight; to see the heavens darkened over him . . . and to see that all this is because of our sins is to see clearly the holy justice and wrath of God against sin. Supremely in Christ do we learn this great truth that God hates sin and judges it with a dreadful and fearful punishment.[6]

Third, Paul's teaching tells us that *God is filled with mercy and love.* In verse 4 he says, "But God, being rich in mercy, because of the great love with which he loved us." This is the *why* of the Christian message. What can explain a gospel that is all of God, in which hopeless sinners find grace in the hands of the holy God they have offended? The answer is found in 1 John 4:8, "God is love." The answer is found in Exodus 34, after Moses had asked the Lord to see his glory. God hid him in a cleft of the rock and passed by, saying, "The LORD, the LORD, a God merciful and gracious, slow to anger, and abounding in steadfast love and faithfulness" (Ex. 34:6). This is how the gospel glorifies God instead of shaming him; it shows what God is really like and makes him attractive to those who know him: God's love is great, and he is rich in mercy.

The Scottish minister Alexander Whyte told of an evening when an older minister came to discuss some pastoral matters. When their business was completed, the old man seemed to want to linger and not want the conversation to end. Finally, after discussing the situations of many other people, he asked, seemingly in jest, "Now, sir, have you any word of comfort for an old sinner like me?" Whyte realized that behind the half-smile was a real seriousness and even a deep agony. He wrote later, "It took my breath away. He was an old saint. But he did not know the peace of forgiveness." Not exactly sure what to do, Whyte walked over and sat beside the older minister, opened his Bible to Micah 7:18, and read, "He delights in showing mercy."

"He delights in showing mercy." Do you remember the atheist's tract complaining about how God could fellowship with scoundrels like those found in the Bible? This is the answer. Yes, Abraham was a coward and idolater. But God delights in showing mercy, so Abraham was called to walk with God and become our forerunner in faith. Jacob was a liar and a cheat. But God delights in mercy, so Jacob became a man of integrity and the father of God's people. Moses was a man of violence. But God delights in mercy, so he called Moses to be his ambassador and lawgiver. Moses became, the Scripture says, the meekest of all the men on the earth (Num. 12:3). David was an adulterer and murderer. But God, who is rich in mercy, enabled him to repent, just as he will allow you to repent and be forgiven. David prayed, "Have mercy on me, O God, according to your steadfast love; according to your abundant mercy blot out my transgressions" (Ps. 51:1). God had mercy on David and restored him to himself.

That was Whyte's answer to the suffering old minister: "He delights in showing mercy." The next morning he received a letter in reply. It read: "Dear friend, I will never doubt Him again. Guilt had hold of me. I was near the gates of Hell, but that word of God comforted me, and I will never doubt Him again. I will never despair again. If the devil casts my sin in my teeth, I will say, 'Yes, it is all true, and you cannot tell the half of it, but I have to deal with the One who delights in showing mercy.' "[7]

This is the God revealed in Paul's teaching of the gospel. As the psalmist sang, "Who is like the Lord our God, who is seated on high, who looks far down on the heavens and the earth? He raises the poor from the dust and lifts the needy from the ash heap, to make them sit with princes, with the princes of his people" (Ps. 113:5–8). "Who is a God like you," the prophet Micah exults, "pardoning iniquity and passing over transgression for the remnant of his inheritance? He does not retain his anger forever, because he delights in steadfast love" (Mic. 7:18).

The Christian Life

These two words, "But God," describe not merely how we are saved at first but also how we live our whole lives as believers. It is by God's action and intervention and prompting all through our lives, to which we respond in faith, that he leads us in the way of new life and ultimately brings us home to heaven.

The life of Abraham clearly shows this progression as well. Abraham was living as a pagan in Ur of the Chaldeans. *But God* called him to journey into a distant land of promise. Abraham believed God and set out on his trip. Before he got to Canaan, however, Abraham settled down in Haran, only partway there. *But God* came back and prodded him forward. Abraham went to Canaan and then a famine struck, so he headed down to Egypt. It was there that he embarrassed himself by having his wife taken in by Pharaoh in order to save his own skin. Things were going badly, "*but the Lord* afflicted Pharaoh and his house with great plagues because of Sarai" (Gen. 12:17). God was working in Abraham's life, and Pharaoh gave Abraham great riches to take his wife away. Abraham returned to Canaan, but grew disconsolate because God had promised to give the land to his descendants, and Abraham did not have a single son. *But God* came to him and showed him the stars in the sky, encouraging his faith with a promise that his offspring would be as numerous as the lights of heaven.

Yet Abraham grew tired of waiting, so he took Sarah's maidservant and had a son with her. This tore his household in two, and Hagar and her son were unjustly sent out into the desert. *But God* found Hagar and preserved her from Abraham's folly. Abraham and Sarah despaired of bearing God's promised son, with Abraham nearing a hundred years old and Sarah being ninety. *But God* sent his angel to renew the promise and open Sarah's womb, so she gave birth to a child, Isaac.

After this great blessing, Abraham was in danger of becoming complacent, *but God* came to him with a new challenge. God directed him to take his son Isaac and offer him as a sacrifice. Abraham, by now, had learned to trust the Lord, so he obeyed. On Mount Moriah, at the spot where Solomon would later build the temple, Abraham raised the knife to kill his beloved son and heir. *But God* sent an angel, who called out, "Abraham, Abraham! . . . Do not lay your hand on the boy" (Gen. 22:11–12), and God provided a ram to be sacrificed in Isaac's place (v. 13). Finally, Abraham grew old and died. His body was placed in the grave, his life on earth having come to an end. *But God* received his spirit, and we know that Abraham entered into the paradise of God, where now he lives forever in glory.

Do you see what this shows? The whole Christian life is a glorious adventure, with God as our Savior and Lord, Teacher and Guide. God calls you to faith, and you have no idea where God is leading you; you cannot imagine how the changes the Bible talks about could happen in your life. The answer is here—"But God." The problems are not really yours but God's, and he is more than able to accomplish all his desire in your life.

You realize, for instance, that you yourself could never become a man of spiritual stature, of solid faith, of self-control and godly dignity. But God can make you such a man. You know that you yourself could never become a woman of inward, spiritual beauty, a bearer of virtue and a source of redeeming love for others. But God can make you such a woman as you trust in him and walk in his ways.

This is the whole Christian life, a journey of discovery into the workings and wonders of God. God intervenes and directs, coaxes and chastises, inspires and empowers. God challenges us and renews our weary souls. He provides the encouragement we need. He convicts our sin. He tests and strengthens our faith. And in the end he makes us vessels of his glory, so that we can say with Paul, "We have this treasure in jars of clay, to show that the surpassing power belongs to God and not to us" (2 Cor. 4:7).

The point is that God is sufficient to meet our every need. Are we ignorant of God and his truth? The fact is that apart from God, we are. Paul writes, "'No eye has seen, no ear has heard, no mind has conceived what God has prepared for those who love him'—*but God* has revealed it to us by his Spirit" (1 Cor. 2:9–10 NIV, quoting Isa. 64:4).

Are we tempted? Certainly we are. "Temptation . . . is common to man; *but God* is faithful, who will not allow you to be tempted beyond what you are able, but with the temptation will also make the way of escape, that you may be able to bear it" (1 Cor. 10:13 NKJV).

Are we weak and foolish? Yes, we are. "*But God* chose what is foolish in the world to shame the wise; God chose what is weak in the world to shame the strong; God chose what is low and despised in the world, even things that are not, to bring to nothing things that are, so that no human being might boast in the presence of God" (1 Cor. 1:27–29).

Are we, or will we be, victimized by the sins of other people? Yes, we can be sure of that happening at some time or another. The Bible says, however, "You intended to harm me, *but God* intended it for good to accomplish what is now being done" (Gen. 50:20 NIV).

James Montgomery Boice therefore concludes, "May I put it quite simply? If you understand those two words—'but God'—they will save your soul. If you recall them daily and live by them, they will transform your life completely."[8]

Those two words also help us to realize that we may safely follow God's Word all the days of our lives. Let us, then, respond in faith to all that he does in and through our lives. Let us give all the glory to God, in whose sovereign grace we rest our hope. And let us live with the truth that the psalmist wrote, "My flesh and my heart may fail, *but God* is the strength of my heart and my portion forever" (Ps. 73:26).

Questions for Study and Reflection

1. Is the sinfulness of the Bible's heroes a scandal? If not, why not? Why do some people think that it is?

2. How do the words "But God" help us understand what the gospel is *not*? What are some common misconceptions that you have heard regarding the gospel?
3. What does "But God" tell us about God himself?
4. Why is it that Paul especially emphasizes God's mercy and grace?
5. Does God's sovereignty rule out our participation in the Christian life? How do divine sovereignty and human responsibility work together?

4

Spiritual Resurrection

Ephesians 2:4–5

But God, being rich in mercy, because of the great love with which he loved us, even when we were dead in our trespasses, made us alive together with Christ—by grace you have been saved.
—Ephesians 2:4–5

If I were asked to summarize the apostle Paul's message in the book of Ephesians, I would not hesitate to say that one major emphasis comes through in everything he is saying in this letter. Paul wants his reader to know that to become a Christian is to be fundamentally changed as a person. A Christian is fundamentally different from a non-Christian and different from the person he or she was before coming to Christ in faith. The changes effected by Christ are not on the periphery of a person but at the very center, changing his basic identity, his nature, and his essence. Perhaps the verse that best sums up Paul's message in Ephesians is found in 2 Corinthians 5:17: "If anyone is in Christ, he is a new creation. The old has passed away; behold, the new has come." That is what Ephesians is all about.

Becoming a Christian is not like joining a country club or taking up a hobby or even undertaking a career change. All these things affect one area of your life but not the others. They are add-ons that do not define who you really are. They are activities to which you devote a certain amount of your life, whereas Christ is your life if you are in him. "For to me, to live is Christ," Paul insists (Phil. 1:21).

Of course, all of us are imperfectly committed to the Lord. But according to Paul's teaching, anyone who treats Christianity as just one compartment of his life, or whose essential person is unchanged by his faith, simply is not a Christian and is not saved. Furthermore, this is true not merely of some Christians—those who are especially devout or committed—but of all Christians. You are not a Christian at all unless an essential change has happened in the core of your person. Martyn Lloyd-Jones writes:

> If [Christianity] is not controlling the whole of your life, then you are just not a Christian. Christians are not people of whom it can be said that their lives are identical with everybody else's, but they have an extra something in addition. . . . No, to be a Christian, says Paul, means that at the very centre, at the very core of your being and existence, this new something has come in and controls everything.[1]

Life from the Dead

In Ephesians 2:5, Paul defines what has happened to a Christian in the most radical terms possible: "When we were dead in our trespasses, [God] made us alive together with Christ." Paul teaches that the change that happens to a Christian is as radical as life from the dead. It is impossible to imagine a more fundamental or comprehensive change than that.

According to Paul, and the Bible as a whole, conversion to Christ involves a spiritual resurrection. You were dead—dead in sins, dead to God, dead in condemnation—but God has given you life. What has happened to us spiritually is what happened when Jesus stood before the tomb and cried, "Lazarus, come out" (John 11:43). Lazarus rose from the grave, and Jesus commanded that his graveclothes be removed. This is what has happened spiritually to all whom Jesus calls to his salvation.

Our spiritual rebirth is analogous to what happened in the creation of the world. It is a re-creation and follows the pattern of the first creation. Genesis 1 tells us that God created all things by his Word, and likewise Peter says to believers, "You have been born again . . . through the living and abiding word of God" (1 Peter 1:23). Furthermore, we are told that in the first creation "the Spirit of God was hovering over the face of the waters" (Gen. 1:2). In the same manner, God's Spirit applies God's Word to our hearts and animates our spirits with a new principle of life.

The result of this regeneration is that we are made anew; we pass from death to life. We should think of this renewal in two simultaneous ways: both judicially and spiritually. Judicially—that is, legally—as we stand before God's throne of judgment, believers pass from death to life. Jesus proclaims in John 5:24, "Truly, truly, I say to you, whoever hears my word and believes him who sent me has eternal life. He does not come into judgment, but has passed from death to life." Paul says in verse 5 that we were "dead in our trespasses," and in verse 3, "children of wrath." Though we have merited death through our sins, Christ has cleansed us by his death, and we are justified through faith in him. We deserved death, but Christ nailed our sins to his cross and granted us life through the gift of his perfect righteousness imputed to us through faith alone.

But Christianity involves more than a legal change of status; to be saved means far more than to be forgiven. We were legally under the curse of death, but our very natures were also spiritually dead, unresponsive to God. Now we have been made spiritually alive to God in Christ. Lloyd-Jones explains: "Regeneration is an act of God by which a principle of new life is implanted in man, and the governing disposition of the soul is made holy. . . . God by His mighty action puts a new disposition into my soul."[2]

The rebirth does not give us new faculties. We had a brain before we were reborn; we have a brain now. We had souls, we had a will, we had a body, and all of that remains true. We also had certain talents, abilities, and experiences, and we retain them as Christians. But a new governing principle is made alive at the very center of our being. Our spirits, which were dead to God, are regenerated and made alive to him. The old faculties and abilities are governed in a new way so that, while we remain ourselves, everything has changed. James Montgomery Boice shows how this renewal changes every aspect of our lives:

> When God breathes new spiritual life into us in the work known as regeneration, we become something we were not before. We have a new life. That life is responsive to the one who gave it. Before this, the Bible meant nothing to us when we read it or it was read in

> our hearing. Now the Bible is intensely alive and interesting. We hear the voice of God in it. Before this, we had no interest in God's people . . . Now they are our very best friends and co-workers. We love their company and cannot seem to get enough of it. Before this, coming to church was boring. Now we are alive to God's presence in the service. Our worship times are the very best times of the week. Before this, service to others and witnessing to the lost seemed strange and senseless, even repulsive. Now they are our chief delight. What has made the difference? The difference is ourselves. God has changed us. We have become alive to him. We are new creatures.[3]

This is not something optional for the front-line Christians. These are not things that are true merely for those who will rise to leadership positions in the church. Ultimately, there is no two-tier Christianity. This enlivening is something that all Christians have experienced, and know they have experienced. Our Lord Jesus said to the Pharisee Nicodemus, "Unless one is born again he cannot see the kingdom of God" (John 3:3). Nicodemus was puzzled at the idea of entering his mother's womb a second time, but Jesus assured him that it was a spiritual rebirth. "That which is born of the flesh is flesh, and that which is born of the Spirit is spirit," the Savior replied. "You must be born again" (3:6–7).

The new birth is necessary to salvation; you cannot be forgiven, you cannot be changed, and you cannot enter into heaven unless, as Paul says in Ephesians 2:5, you who were dead in trespasses are made alive together with Christ.

So how do you know that you are born again, that you have passed from death to life? The most essential answer is that it is by the new birth that sinners repent and believe on Jesus Christ. It is by the Word and God's Spirit that anyone truly believes, so that those who trust in Christ are born again and enter a new life in which all the other blessings of salvation are certain to follow.

Dead to Sin, Alive to God

When the New Testament speaks about our spiritual resurrection, it always speaks in two ways. The first is that those who are born again are *dead to sin.* That is, a new life has begun and the end has come to our former life that was dead in sin.

Perhaps Paul's clearest teaching on this first point is found in Romans 6. There, he challenges the idea that God's grace could lead to a life that continues in sin: "Are we to continue in sin that grace may abound? By no means! How can we who died to sin still live in it?" Just as Jesus died on the cross for our sins, by union with him in faith we too have died to sin, "in order that, just as Christ was raised from the dead by the glory of the Father, we too might walk in newness of life" (Rom. 6:1–4).

The implication of the new birth is that *we must no longer live as we did before.* We are no longer what we were; our old life has ended, and therefore we must no longer try to live in the old manner. We can never go back to the old life—in fact, if we try to live in the old way, we only make a mockery of ourselves. God's Spirit lives in us now, so we cannot prosper in the ways of sin. An adult cannot become a child again, but he can disgrace himself with childish behavior. Likewise, as Christians, the only thing for us to do is to renounce the old life of sin, the end of which was death, and embrace the reality that we are no longer to live as we formerly did. John Stott puts it this way:

> Our biography is written in two volumes. Volume one is the story of the old man, the old self, of me before

> my conversion. Volume two is the story of the new man, the new self, of me after I was made a new creation in Christ. Volume one of my biography ended with the judicial death of the old self. I was a sinner. I deserved to die. I did die. I received my deserts in my Substitute with whom I have become one. Volume two of my biography opened with my resurrection. My old life having finished, a new life to God has begun.[4]

This takes us directly to the second reality involved in our having been brought from death to life by God. Christians are dead to sin and also *alive to God.* The rebirth is the beginning of the spiritual life of walking with God in righteousness, truth, and love. Paul puts the two realities together in Romans 6:11: "So you also must consider yourselves dead to sin and alive to God in Christ Jesus." We need to know this, lest we be tempted to return to the former ways of sin and death.

God has done for us what Hernando Cortez did for the Spanish explorers who landed in Mexico. As soon as they arrived in the New World, Cortez burned the ships that might take them back to their former life. With the ships destroyed, his army had nowhere to go but forward into a new life.

That is exactly what God has done for us in Christ. We cannot pretend not to have the Holy Spirit dwelling in us and convicting us of sin. We cannot deny or reject the authority of the God we have come to know. We cannot keep God's Word from stirring up our hearts and enlightening our minds. The life of spiritual death is behind us—and praise the Lord for that. We are alive to God, and now we are to live for him. Paul therefore commands us:

> Let not sin therefore reign in your mortal body, to make you obey its passions. Do not present your

> members to sin as instruments for unrighteousness, but present yourselves to God as those who have been brought from death to life, and your members to God as instruments for righteousness. For sin will have no dominion over you, since you are not under law but under grace. (Rom. 6:12–14)

This means that we are to offer our eyes to God, no longer sinning in lust or envy or otherwise watching sinful things, but using them to bring godly images into our minds. We are to offer our lips to God, making our speech a source of blessing and salvation, instead of, as James 3:8 puts it, the "restless evil, full of deadly poison" that used to characterize our speech. We are to offer our feet to God, so that they take us into places of worship and ministry rather than of sin and folly. We are to offer our hands to God, helping those in need and lifting up those who are fallen. This is the new life to which we have been saved; it could not be more practical.

Because of the new birth, Christians are dead to the old life of sin and must no longer live as we did before. But this is combined with the wonderful news that Christians are now alive to God. This means not only that we *must* not live as we did before, but that we *may* not live as we did before. *Combined with a new obligation is a new ability.* We are able in Christ to do what we could never do before. Why? Because the power of God is now working in our lives. This is the point of Paul's analogy between our rebirth and the resurrection of Jesus. Our new life is energized by the same power that raised Jesus from the grave, conveyed to us by the Word and through prayer. Therefore, things that are naturally beyond our power are now possible to us in the supernatural power of God. "My grace is sufficient for you," God promises, "for my power is made perfect in weakness" (2 Cor. 12:9). Therefore, Paul boasted, "I can do all things through him who strengthens me" (Phil. 4:13).

Do you realize, if you have come to faith in Christ, that God's own power is available for your growth in grace and godliness? When you pray, asking for strength to turn from sin or to grow in godly character, God's power flows to you through the channel of your faith and by the ministry of his Holy Spirit. Paul writes in 1 Corinthians 4:20, "The kingdom of God does not consist in talk but in power." The availability of Christ's resurrection power is the cause of our boldness in the Christian life; this is why we can aspire to purity and godly love. For as Paul wrote to young Timothy, "God gave us a spirit not of fear but of power and love and self-control" (2 Tim. 1:7).

Jesus and Nicodemus

I mentioned Jesus' teaching to Nicodemus in John 3, one of the Bible's most important passages on the spiritual rebirth. Nicodemus came to Jesus at the beginning of our Lord's ministry, after Jesus had taught and performed miracles in Jerusalem. Nicodemus represented everything the world admires, everything in which a man might place his confidence for salvation. John 3:1 introduces him as "a man of the Pharisees . . . , a ruler of the Jews." The Pharisees were those most admired by the people for their religious piety. No one performed more and better religious works than people such as Nicodemus. Furthermore, he was "a ruler of the Jews" (John 3:1). He was a member of the Sanhedrin, the highest ruling body among the Jews in that day. Moreover, we can be sure that Nicodemus was also a scholar. All Pharisees were devoted students of Scripture. Given his Greek name, Nicodemus must also have come from a family that studied the philosophers. What more could a man be than this? It is hard to pick a similar figure from our own time who combines all of this: religious devotion, political power, ethical excellence, and erudite scholarship.

This is the man who came to Jesus. John tells us that he came by night, no doubt to avoid being seen consulting Jesus of Nazareth, a mere carpenter-turned-rabbi. But Nicodemus saw something he admired in Jesus: "Rabbi, we know that you are a teacher come from God, for no one can do these signs that you do unless God is with him" (John 3:2). It seems that Nicodemus was offering his considerable help to Jesus' ministry. If Jesus were just a human rabbi, I am sure he would have accepted; the partnership of such a man could mean access, recognition, political pull, and financial support.

But Jesus was not just another human teacher, and he was not impressed by either Nicodemus or his offer of assistance. Jesus replied, "Truly, truly, I say to you, unless one is born again he cannot see the kingdom of God" (John 3:3). This was Jesus' message to such a man as Nicodemus, just as it is his message to everyone who thinks to be saved by his pedigree or power, by popularity or good works or petty morality.

What are you bringing to Jesus for your salvation? Do you, like so many other people, expect God to accept you as "a basically good person"? If so, Jesus will convict you of the reality of your sin and demand that you confess your need of his grace. Do you offer the clean hands of supposedly good works? Then Jesus will point to the spots that your eyes do not see. He will tell you to clean out the inside of your heart, where filthy things live and flourish. Whatever works or human merit you bring to God, expecting to be commended and accepted in the holy courts of heaven, Jesus says to you as to Nicodemus, "You must be born again."

This is something that Paul, too, had to learn. He once boasted in similar sources of self-righteousness, things that he considered spiritual assets—his bloodline, his upbringing, his circumcision, his religious works and morality, his hatred of God's enemies. But when God opened his eyes, he realized, "Whatever gain I had, I counted as loss for the sake of Christ.

Indeed, I count . . . them as rubbish, in order that I may gain Christ and be found in him, not having a righteousness of my own that comes from the law, but that which comes through faith in Christ . . .—that I may know him and the power of his resurrection" (Phil. 3:7–10). Just as Paul realized, and just as Jesus demanded of Nicodemus, whoever you are you must repent of your former life, of your claims to merit before God, laying hold instead of God's grace in Jesus Christ—by which you, a sinner, may be born again.

Saved by Grace

This is the very idea with which Paul completes verse 5: "By grace you have been saved." We hear a lot about grace, but here we find what it really means to be saved by grace alone.

To be saved by grace means, first of all, that *you do not deserve what God has granted to you.* It is not something that happens because of what you are or what you have done—but in spite of what you are and what you have done. *Grace* is often defined as "God's unmerited favor." That is true, but it does not go far enough. Grace is God's favor to those who have merited his wrath. Paul says, "We were dead in our trespasses"; we were at war with God and under God's just condemnation. But by his sheer grace alone—not because of something in you but because of something in him, because, as verse 4 says, "God [is] rich in mercy, because of the great love with which he loved us"—God saved you when you deserved to be condemned, when you were unable even to lift a finger to believe and come to God. As Paul writes in Titus 3:5–6, "He saved us, not because of works done by us in righteousness, but according to his own mercy, by the washing of regeneration and renewal of the Holy Spirit, whom he poured out on us richly through Jesus Christ our Savior."

Second, grace means that *you did not achieve salvation by any power within yourself* but by the resurrection power of God working in your life. God "made us alive" when we were dead—this, too, is what it means to be saved by grace.

Having been saved by grace, we continue to live by grace. Christians do not grow through their own effort or their own inner strength, but through the grace of God that works mightily in our lives through God's Word and prayer. Therefore, the Christian who wants to grow in his or her faith, to bear the spiritual fruit that is of God, will be devoted to studying the Bible and will regularly draw near to God in prayer.

Third, this passage tells us that *to be saved by grace is to be joined to the Lord Jesus Christ through faith.* It was "together with Christ" that God made us alive. It is because Christ died for us and rose again for us that we die to our old lives and live anew to God, as Christ's redeeming power works through every area of our lives.

THE TWO *MUSTS*

I think back to Jesus' teaching to Nicodemus: "You must be born again" (John 3:7). But he made a second statement in John chapter 3 that also centers on the word *must.* When Nicodemus asked how this could be, Jesus replied, "The Son of Man [must] be lifted up, that whoever believes in him may have eternal life" (3:14–15). When Jesus told Nicodemus that he needed to be born again, Jesus knew that first he needed to die on the cross for our sins.

Nicodemus didn't understand this at first, and he departed from our Lord. But he shows up again in John's Gospel. In John 7 we are told that he spoke up for Jesus before the Sanhedrin and was criticized for sympathizing with Jesus. He still stood apart from Christ, trusting his political and religious credentials, though God was calling in his heart and Nicodemus was starting to listen. As often happens, the new birth did not take place without God's having worked for some time in his life.

The day came, however, when what Jesus had spoken of actually happened: the Son of Man was lifted up on the cross. Nicodemus was there, and as he stood by and watched, he surely remembered Jesus' words: "You must be born again . . . The Son of Man [must] be lifted up" (John 3:7, 14). Finally, then, the scholar and politician and religious leader saw the kingdom of God. He saw Jesus on the cross as the Savior of his own soul; he saw his own redemption by the shedding of Christ's precious blood; and by God's grace, through faith, he was born again.

John 19:38–39 tells us what happened. After Jesus' death, "Joseph of Arimathea, who was a disciple of Jesus, . . . asked Pilate that he might take away the body of Jesus, and Pilate gave him permission. . . . Nicodemus also, who earlier had come to Jesus by night, came bringing a mixture of myrrh and aloes. . . ." Finally Nicodemus came out into the light with his commitment to Jesus. He cast aside his reputation among the religious and scholarly and political elite. He turned his back on fame and wealth and the lifestyle they might offer him and turned in faith to the crucified Jesus Christ, willing to be his disciple, come what may, beginning a new life, dead to sin and alive to God together with Christ. "So it is," Jesus had said to him on that fateful first night's meeting, "with everyone who is born of the Spirit" (John 3:8).

The Son of Man must be lifted up on the cross because you must be born again. And it is by believing that Jesus died for your sins, and that he rose again to grant you eternal life, that you, like Nicodemus, even when you were dead in trespasses, are made alive together with Christ.

Questions for Study and Reflection

1. The author states that "Paul wants us to know that to become a Christian is to be fundamentally changed as a person." What are some of the ways that becoming a Christian changes us?

2. How does a believer's re-creation in Christ resemble the original creation of the world? How is our new birth like Lazarus' resurrection from the grave? What do these examples tell us about Christian salvation?
3. How does Christian salvation involve *judicial* new life? How does it involve *spiritual* new life? How are these two related?
4. The New Testament says that Christians are now dead to sin. How does this work out in our experience? How is it working out in your personal experience?
5. The author states that through our new birth, Christians receive new abilities and power that enable us to overcome sin. What are some of these new abilities? How do we gain spiritual power to defeat sin? What is the source of our spiritual power as Christians?

5

Together with Christ

Ephesians 2:5–6

Even when we were dead in our trespasses, [God] made us alive together with Christ—by grace you have been saved—and raised us up with him and seated us with him in the heavenly places in Christ Jesus.
—Ephesians 2:5–6

The nineteenth-century Scotsman Hugh Martin wrote that Christianity can be summed up in two expressions: "Christ for Us" and "We with Christ."[1] This perfectly encapsulates Paul's thought in Ephesians chapters 1 and 2. Chapter 1 tells what God has done for us in Christ, apart from which we cannot be saved. The New Testament proclaims this doctrine over and over: Christ was made sin for us (2 Cor. 5:21); he was made a curse for us (Gal. 3:13); he died for us (Rom. 5:8); he rose from the grave for us (Rom. 8:34; 2 Cor. 5:15); and he ascended into heaven and rules in power for us (Eph. 1:22). Everything Jesus did, he did for us, that we might be saved.

But as Martin points out, "Christ for Us" must be joined to "We with Christ." We must receive Christ and trust him for our salvation and become his disciple. Therefore, the New Testament proclaims, we were "crucified with Christ" (Gal. 2:20). And as Paul teaches in Ephesians 2:5–6, we were made alive with Christ, and raised with Christ, and seated with Christ in heavenly places. Martin explains, "If he lived for us, we now live with him, for as he was, so are we in the world."[2] Jesus' experience has become our experience. Just as he died for our sin, we now die to our sin with him. Just as he was resurrected to live with God forever, so we now also live a new life in service to God.

Union with Christ

This is the great doctrine of the believer's union with Jesus Christ. Arthur Pink wrote, "The subject of spiritual union is the most important, the most profound, and yet the most blessed of any that is set forth in sacred Scripture." But then he lamented, "Sad to say, there is hardly any [subject] which is now more generally neglected. The very expression 'spiritual union' is unknown in most professing Christian circles."[3]

What, then, does it mean to be united with Christ? Paul explains the concept with three statements found in verses 5 and 6. He says in verse 5 that believers are "made . . . alive together with Christ." He adds in verse 6 that we were also "raised . . . up with him" and "seated . . . with him." These three expressions sum up Paul's understanding of what it means to have union with Christ through faith.

It is helpful to know that Paul coined three new words in this description. The union with Christ of which he speaks was a new reality that had not previously been known, so no suitable words were available. Just as people today come up with new words as needed, such as *Internet* and *networking*, Paul, too, invented new words. His new words here each involve a combination using the Greek prefix *syn*, which means "together with." For the first, he combines the verb for *to live* (Greek, *zōein*) with the verb for *to make* (Greek, *poiein*), and adds the prefix *with*. His new word is *made alive together with* (Greek, *synezōopoiēsen*). The second and third words are simpler ones: Paul adds *with* to the word for *to raise up* (Greek, *synēgeiren*), and also to the verb that means "to be seated" (Greek, *synekathisen*): made alive with, raised up with, and seated with.

With these three words, Paul expresses the believer's union with Christ. But what kind of union is it? Our union with Christ is obviously not a physical one; we were not physically dead, and we have not physically been raised up to heaven.

The Bible speaks of our union with Christ in two senses. The first is a covenant or representative union. It is often called "federal headship." When we receive Jesus as our Savior, we become the beneficiaries of all that he did; our sins are credited to him to be put away on the cross, and his righteousness is credited to us. This is what Martin's expression "Christ for Us" gets at—believers are joined to Christ in God's saving covenant so that we receive the benefit of what Jesus did. Jesus came into the world with a work to be done, and as he died on the cross, he cried out in satisfaction, "It is finished" (John 19:30). Those who are joined to him by faith are represented by Christ and his work before God.

But that is not the only kind of union of which the Bible speaks. There is also the believer's spiritual or experiential union with Christ. This is Paul's emphasis in these verses. He means that the experience of Jesus in his death, resurrection, ascension, and heavenly reign sets the pattern for our experience on earth and then in heaven. God's Son became like us so that we might become like him. This is what Paul means when he writes, "I have been crucified with Christ. It is no longer I who live, but Christ who lives in me" (Gal. 2:20).

This spiritual union is what defines a true Christian. A Christian is not merely someone who comes to church and who even assents to certain doctrines. A Christian is one in whom Christ is living, and whose life is increasingly taking on Christ's pattern of death, resurrection, ascension to heaven, and eternal reign. Everything Paul speaks of in these verses is described in the past tense: having died with Christ, a believer has been made alive with Christ, raised up with Christ, and seated with him in the heavenly realms.

Verses 5 and 6 involve ideas that are difficult to understand, until we realize that Paul is contrasting our present experience with his description of our past in verses 1–3. There is a parallelism that unlocks the meaning of Paul's three invented words. Paul said that we were "dead in our trespasses"; now he says that we have been "made alive together with Christ." He said that we were in bondage to the world, the devil, and the flesh; now he says that we have been raised up into a heavenly citizenship. He said that we were "by nature children of wrath." But we are no longer under God's condemnation and have been seated with Christ in the heavenly realms.

Made Alive Together in Christ

The first of these terms describes what has happened to us in our conversion to Christ as a spiritual resurrection.[4] We were "dead in our trespasses," but God has "made us alive together with Christ." We were uninterested in the things of God;

now we find them exciting and important. We were unresponsive to God's promptings and repulsed by the Bible, but now we find ourselves being molded by God's Word and eager to learn more of the Bible's teaching. We never used to pray, except out of desperation; now we talk with God all the time. What has happened? Just as God raised Jesus from the dead, he has made us spiritually alive. We were living as if God did not exist, or, like Adam and Eve after their sin, we were trying to escape from God. But now, not only do we know that God is there, but we trust him as our Lord and Savior.

I recently read of a conversion example that is probably more dramatic than most. In 1997, Brian Deegan formed the Metal Mulisha freestyle motocross team. Over the next eight years, Deegan and his friends won numerous motorcycle races and jumping competitions, while establishing their reputation for mayhem, destruction, and violence. Their lifestyle was emblemized by their tattoos and Nazi symbolism, and consisted mainly of motorcycles, alcohol, drugs, sex, and riots. But three things happened to Brian Deegan that led to a radical change. The first was that his girlfriend became pregnant and insisted on keeping their child. The second was a failed attempt at a high-speed midair backflip that very nearly ended Deegan's life and led to months of rehabilitation. The third was his agreement to attend church with his girlfriend. To his surprise, he didn't hate it, and before long he had come to saving faith in Jesus. As a result, he married his girlfriend and quit drinking and drugs; another result was that he invited his fellow Metal Mulisha bikers to study the Bible with him. One by one they were all born again to faith in Jesus. "He kept telling us how much the Bible changed his life," one recalled. "I felt like I had to listen." Today, Metal Mulisha's tattooed riders still win motocross championships, but an inner transformation has taken place that is working out in their lives. Deegan, once the epitome of the angry, foulmouthed insurrectionist, now sits with a Bible open on his lap and tells sports journalists that he wants his daughter to be able to look up to his example as a Christian father.[5] Having been very publicly dead in sin, he is now alive to God in Jesus Christ.

Martyn Lloyd-Jones uses the illustration of a flower that is closed up at night, its petals turned inward and its face closed to God. That is how our hearts and minds were with respect to God. But the sun comes up in the morning, and its glorious rays strike the flower's petals. What happens? The petals open toward the sun and soak in its life-giving rays. That is what God has done with us.[6] Paul says in 2 Corinthians 4:6 that God "has shone in our hearts to give the light of the knowledge of the glory of God in the face of Jesus Christ." We are now alive to God, and our lives are turned to him for light and salvation in Jesus Christ. That is what it means to be born again, to be made alive to God together with Christ.

Raised Up with Christ

According to Paul, the life that was dead in sin had two chief features. There were two sides to our problem: our guilt and our bondage. Speaking of sin's bondage, he said that we were "following the course of this world, following the prince of the power of the air . . . in the passions of our flesh, carrying out the desires of the body and the mind" (Eph. 2:2–3). If the life in sin involves that kind of bondage, then salvation in Christ means deliverance and liberation. Paul refers to this concept in his second description of our union with Christ, writing in verse 6 that God "raised us up with him."

This description refers to Jesus' ascension into heaven and its significance for believers. Jesus was taken out of this world and entered into his heavenly life. Likewise, we who are still physically in this world are no longer of it, but begin our own heavenly life. We are no longer slaves to the thoughts and desires of the world. We are no longer in bondage to the prince of this present evil age—that is, the devil. We are no longer powerless before the temptations of sinful desires. Just as Christ ascended into heaven, we, too, are no longer ruled by worldly powers but are under authority of the kingdom of God.

In Philippians 3:18–21, Paul explains this doctrine by contrasting the one who belongs to this world and the Christian, whose citizenship is now in heaven. Of the worldly person, he writes, "Their end is destruction, their god is their belly, and they glory in their shame, with minds set on earthly things." But a Christian's "citizenship is in heaven, and from it we await a Savior, the Lord Jesus Christ, who will transform our lowly body to be like his glorious body, by the power that enables him even to subject all things to himself."

This is the difference between a Christian and the man or woman of the world. The worldly man worships "his belly," Paul observes; that is, he worships those things that satisfy his fleshly cravings. Furthermore, he glories in things that are shameful, having his mind set on earthly things. That is a perfect description of the values and ideals of this present world, along with those who belong to it. But a Christian is one who has been spiritually taken out of the world. His citizenship is in heaven, and the things he hopes for are there, safe and secure with Christ. He does not look forward to worldly riches or glory or fame or pleasure, but has set his hope on a heavenly reward. Paul adds that he awaits the return of Jesus Christ and the final resurrection. That is the salvation he seeks.

This is something that God has done to and for everyone who is joined to Christ in faith. This is not just a qualification for top Christians, but is the basic description of everyone who is truly joined to Christ and is saved. It is not optional, but fundamental to Christianity. For sure, the implications are still being worked out in our lives. This is what Christian growth and maturity look like: we think less and less like the world around us. Worldly affairs and pleasures occupy less of our attention, and we think more about Christ and heaven. We are like a person who has his home address and his business address on his calling card. Heaven is our home; this present world is just our place of business for the time being. Our thoughts, our desires, our affections are increasingly geared toward being with Christ in heaven. We are in the world, but no longer of it. The apostle John therefore writes, "Do not love the world or the things in the world. If anyone loves the world, the love of the Father is not in him. For all that is in the world—the desires of the flesh and the desires of the eyes and pride in possessions—is not from the Father but is from the world" (1 John 2:15–16).

People complain about this kind of Christianity. You hear it said, "That person is too heavenly-minded to be of earthly good." I have found that statement to have it exactly backward. It is the heavenly-minded people who are the most earthly good—who are most merciful and who give sacrificially to others and to God's work in the world. Instead, it is the earthly-minded person who is of little heavenly good! It is the man or woman whose heart is still attached to worldly status symbols and worldly entertainments, to worldly boasting and worldly ambitions, who has little or no time to serve the kingdom of God or to sacrifice for the blessing of other people.

The true Christian, Paul proclaims, has been raised up together with Christ. There is no other way to serve and worship God. We cannot look up and look down at the same time. We cannot serve both God and money. We cannot live for this present life and also store up treasures in heaven. Jesus teaches, "Where your treasure is, there your heart will be also" (Matt. 6:21). We can live as if this present life were our ultimate destination, seeking to enrich and fill ourselves with everything we desire, as if there were no God and as if eternity were but a mirage. The Bible calls such a person "Fool!" (Luke 12:20). Or we can believe the Bible's teaching that this life is not our destination, but only preparation for eternity to come. The Christian's destination is in eternity, in heaven, and we must live now as those whose hopes have been raised there together with Christ.

God makes us alive from the death of our sin, and then delivers us from the bondage of a worldly life to live as citizens of heaven and eternal sons and heirs.

Seated with Christ

Third, Paul says that God "seated us with him in the heavenly places in Christ Jesus" (v. 6). This statement refers to Christ's reign in power, seated in heaven at the right hand of God the Father. Believers join in this powerful position, and its effects become real in our present experience.

Following the contrast with verses 1–3, we see that verse 6 corresponds to our condemnation in sin as "children of wrath." In Christ, we are no longer condemned, but are seated with him in the presence of God. The opposite of condemnation and judgment is not just acquittal or forgiveness. We aspire to too little if we think this is all we want from God. The opposite of condemnation is acceptance into God's inner circle, adoption into his family, and being embraced close to his side, to be seated at his right hand together with Christ. God has "seated us with him in the heavenly places in Christ Jesus."

This idea would have been more familiar back in the days of kings and queens. A king would take someone into his favor and allow the man or woman to ride next to him while traveling. The favored person would have intimate fellowship with the king, sharing his thoughts and observations. He would be blessed with the king's attention and affection. This is what it means for us, who were condemned in our guilt, to be made alive with Christ, raised up with him, and then seated with him in the heavenly places.

A helpful example is the medieval story of King Arthur's Round Table. There the king gathered his loyal knights. They sat together for fellowship and council of war, profiting from Arthur's wisdom, and sharing with him his burdens and triumphs. The Bible states that believers will "reign with" Christ (2 Tim. 2:12); we will be his band of brothers, his mighty men and maidens, his trusted comrades in arms.

An early scene in J. R. R. Tolkien's *The Return of the King* makes me think of Paul's teaching. The hero of the story, the mighty wizard Gandalf, arrives at a great city just in time to help defend it from attack. With him is one of the hobbits, the small and insignificant people who play so important a role in the book. When Gandalf and the hobbit arrive, the ruler of the city is fascinated by the small creature, who in turn is awed by the ruler and the glory of his city. A bond between them is forged, and the hobbit offers his fealty to the lord, who takes him into his service as his personal squire. He seats the hobbit beside him on his throne, and during the day the ruler tells him the lore of the kingdom and recounts the great triumphs of his realm. The hobbit, meanwhile, shares with the king the story of his own adventures and sings songs from his native land.

This is a lovely picture of the great privilege that has been granted us by God as he takes us into his service and favor and even into his intimate presence. It reminds me of the apostle John seated next to the Lord Jesus at the Last Supper, resting his head on Jesus' breast. When we celebrate the Lord's Supper, we should realize that we have likewise been seated at the table of Christ's fellowship, to partake of the glorious grace of God. C. Austin Miles wonderfully expressed this truth in a hymn:

And he walks with me, and he talks with me,
And he tells me I am his own;
And the joy we share as we tarry there,
None other has ever known.[7]

Do you know anything about that? Do you know what it is to be seated in the heavenly realms with Christ? Has God disclosed to you something of his glory through his Word? Have you felt the warmth of his interest and fellowship in prayer? This is the Christian life. God opens up his own heart to us and makes our cares his own.

Furthermore, Jesus' sitting down was a sign of his total victory. According to the Bible, God seated Christ above every name and power and placed all his enemies beneath his feet. The same is true for us, being seated with him. As Paul states in Romans 6:14, "Sin will have no dominion over you."

Christians sin, but no longer because we must. The world, the devil, and the flesh may tempt you, but they can no longer rule you. Paul writes in Romans 8:2, "The law of the Spirit of life has set you free in Christ Jesus from the law of sin and death." Just as God raised our Lord Jesus into heaven and seated him at his right hand, so also will God deliver you from the power and persecution and condemnation of this world. As John teaches, "The world is passing away along with its desires, but whoever does the will of God abides forever" (1 John 2:17).

Moreover, being seated with Christ, Christians have full assurance of salvation. God receives us with the promise of his gospel: "For I will be merciful toward their iniquities, and I will remember their sins no more" (Heb. 8:12, quoting Jer. 31:34). Jesus adds, "Come to me, all who labor and are heavy laden, and I will give you rest" (Matt. 11:28). God's Word asks us, seated as we are in Christ, "Who shall bring any charge against God's elect? It is God who justifies. Who is to condemn?

Christ Jesus is the one who died—more than that, who was raised—who is at the right hand of God, who indeed is interceding for us. Who shall separate us from the love of Christ?" (Rom. 8:33–35). Because we rest on Christ's finished work, safe and secure, Paul concludes, "We are more than conquerors through him who loved us" (Rom. 8:37).

Saved by Grace

Paul is describing true Christianity, something far more than mere attendance at church and knowledge of doctrine. This is an exalted life in radical contrast with the life we have known before. We were dead, but God has made us alive. We were slaves to sin, but God has liberated us to live in righteousness, peace, and joy. We were condemned in our guilt, but God has elevated us to the inner circle of his intimate fellowship, to rest and assurance of eternal blessing and life.

Many of us will have to admit that we know little or nothing of what Paul is saying. This is why we need to remember his exclamation right in the middle of this carefully crafted teaching. You can always tell when something is burdening Paul's mind, because he simply cannot hold it in. Here, it slips out at the end of verse 5: "By grace you have been saved."

How important this is for us to remember. When Paul proclaims that God made us alive together with Christ, raised us up with Christ, and seated us with Christ in the heavenly realms, he is not talking about something we have to do. He is not challenging us to get our act together. He is talking about a gift that every Christian has received, yet how few realize the extent of God's grace for us in Christ. Paul's point is not to show you how you are failing and how disappointed God is with you, but rather to open your eyes to how dear you are to God and all that he has made available to you in Christ. This is all past tense. It is accomplished. If you are in Christ through a living faith, then you have been made alive with him, you have been raised up as a citizen of heaven, and you have been seated with Christ in God's presence, clothed with forgiveness and favor and fellowship with God.

William Barclay tells of a Scottish woman who lived in squalor in the cellar of her large house. Shortly after George Matheson arrived as the new pastor of her church, a man stopped by to find that she now lived in the bedroom on the top floor and that all was neat and clean. He commented on the change, and she replied, "Ay, you canna hear George Matheson preach and live in a cellar."[8] So it is with Paul's teaching here. Are you living in the cellar of the salvation that God has provided to you in Christ? Then move up into the rooms that God has long since prepared for you, and begin to live the life that he has made possible for you in Jesus Christ.

If you are not a Christian, then this is what you are missing. You are dead in trespasses, alienated from God and his love, held fast in the bitter chains of a loveless, cruel, and evil world. Even worse, whether you know it or not, you stand condemned in the courts of God's eternal judgment. Here is good news, for if you will confess your sin and look to Jesus Christ for salvation, if you will cry to heaven, where he is seated with God, you will be not only completely forgiven but completely saved. You may be transformed and renewed, liberated from the bondage of your old, rotten life and granted a share in the eternal inheritance of glory.

If you are in Christ, if you have long since believed on Jesus and called on his name, then start receiving by faith the riches that God proclaims to you from this text. You are no longer dead, so start living to God. You are no longer a slave to sin but a citizen of heaven. Start living for things that will never fade away. And you are nearer to the heart of God than you ever imagined, seated with him in Christ. Give him your heart and take his in return. Partake of his glory and then start reflecting his light into a world that is dead in sin, so that others might be saved by the same grace that gave this matchless gift to you.

Questions for Study and Reflection

1. Explain the meaning of the expressions "Christ for Us" and "We with Christ." Explain how these sum up the Christian experience.
2. What does it mean to be united with Christ? How do we gain union with Christ? Explain the two senses of union with Christ that the author mentions.
3. Do you believe that you have been "made alive together with Christ"? If so, what transformations have you been experiencing as a result? What would you say to someone who said that we can be joined to Christ without changing our lives?
4. What does Paul mean by saying that Christians have been "raised up together with Christ"? Can Christians try to lead both worldly and godly lives? Have you tried? If so, what happened?
5. What does Paul mean by saying that Christians have been "seated with Christ"? What is the role of the Bible and of prayer in our daily communion with God?

6

The Glory of God in Salvation

Ephesians 2:7

. . . so that in the coming ages he might show the immeasurable riches of his grace in kindness toward us in Christ Jesus.
—Ephesians 2:7

One of the most challenging features of modern life is the sense of insignificance that so many people feel. What does it matter, they think, at least in the grand scheme of things, how they live or what they contribute in life?

In part, this view is fueled by our society's cult of celebrity. We think fame is what determines a person's significance. Pop artist Andy Warhol predicted that in the future "everyone will be world-famous for fifteen minutes." But most of us will never be famous for even five minutes, so we don't feel very important.

This is all magnified by today's secular ideology, and especially by the theory of evolution, the whole point of which is that there is no God who either created or governs this world. As a result, there is no meaning to life. Harvard professor Stephen Jay Gould sums up the implication of evolutionary atheism this way: "We are here by accident. . . . We have no intrinsic meaning."[1] If that is true, then my job is just to make it through life, to have as many good times and as few bad times as possible, and to succeed in my selfish ambitions.

How does Christianity differ from this point of view? Christianity proclaims that there is a God and that it is unto him that we live. Man, like all the rest of creation, was made by God and for God. As the first question of the Westminster Shorter Catechism so famously tells us, we do have a purpose: "Man's chief end is to glorify God, and to enjoy him forever."

This is bad news to unbelievers because, despite their unbelief, the God who is really there is going to hold them to account. But it is wonderful news to God's people because it means that even though we are ignored or despised by the world, our intense longing for purpose and meaning, a longing that burns deep within our hearts, is fulfilled in the eternal glory of God. Sinclair Ferguson observes, "The average man . . . has accepted the idea that life is without final purpose, and so he naturally devotes himself to whatever interests him at the moment. By contrast the Christian . . . walks on the path which God has laid; he enjoys the purpose for his life which God has ordained; he looks forward to the destiny which God has planned."[2]

God's Glory the Reason for Salvation

In Ephesians 2:7, Paul deals with this matter of meaning and purpose. He has been teaching about the glorious blessings that come to those who belong to Jesus Christ. He has said that having been spiritually dead, we have been made alive. Having been slaves to sin, we have been raised up into the liberty of a heavenly citizenship. Having been condemned in our guilt, we are seated with God in loving fellowship. For many of us, all of this seems too much to believe. Therefore, Paul tells us the reason for such an abundance of blessing for those who were God's enemies before he saved them. God did this, he teaches, "so that in the coming ages he might show the immeasurable riches of his grace in kindness toward us in Christ Jesus."

This statement tells us that *the reason for our salvation is the glory of God.* People hear the gospel and find it hard to believe that God would pardon and renew sinners by the sacrificial death of his Son. Why would God be willing to do this? they ask. The ultimate answer is that our salvation will serve to glorify God forever. Here is a great ground of assurance and hope to Christians who believe God's Word but feel so unworthy of salvation: it is precisely by saving people like us that God glorifies himself; it is precisely by loving his enemies and transforming us into loving children by his grace that God is glorified in our salvation.

In this sense, it is the greatest sinners who provide for God the greatest glory in salvation, so that Paul could boast, "Where sin increased, grace abounded all the more" (Rom. 5:20). That is not an incentive for us to sin, of course, because salvation delivers us from sin. Instead, it is a demonstration of the power of God's grace. In the early days of Christianity, there was no greater enemy to the church than the man who later wrote this letter: Saul of Tarsus, later the apostle Paul. Paul never tired of pointing out how much it glorified God to save a horrible man like him, making Paul a trophy of grace before all the world (see 1 Tim. 1:15–16). It will be the same with you in your great sin, which is conquered by a greater grace.

We need to realize that just as the chief end of man is to glorify God, so also the chief end of God is to glorify himself. This is what God wants: for his glory to be displayed. When we talk about the glory of God, what we mean is the revealing of his perfections, the displaying of his glorious attributes. When we say that God desires his own glory, what we mean is that he wants to reveal who he is, what he is like. It is a sin for us to seek self-glory; indeed, self-glory is the fountainhead of so many of our sins. But God is the One who is worthy above all to be glorified. For God to desire his own glory is not only good, but the highest possible good; for him to be known is for glory to shine. As Paul writes in Romans 11:36, "For from him and through him and to him are all things. To him be glory forever."

This tells us the purpose of creation: God created the universe to display his glory. According to Psalm 19:1, "The heavens declare the glory of God, and the sky above proclaims his handiwork." Old Testament scholar E. J. Young writes, "The entirety of creation . . . speaks with voices clear and positive of the glory of the Holy God. Wherever we turn our eyes, we see the marks of His majesty, and should lift our hearts in praise to Him who is holy. This is His world, the wide theater in which His perfect glory is displayed."[3] The chief end of creation is to glorify God.

The same is true of redemption; in redemption, God achieves all his aims in creation. It was for the sake of God's glory that Jesus was born, lived, died, and rose from the grave. On the night of Jesus' birth, the angels sang, "Glory to God in the highest" (Luke 2:14). On the night of his arrest, Jesus began praying in the garden of Gethsemane in the same fashion: "Father, . . . glorify your Son that the Son may glorify you" (John 17:1).

The same is also true when it comes to the Holy Spirit's work in our lives. Why are we born again? Why are we raised and seated together with Christ? So that God's glory may be seen forever through his grace in our lives.

In the Coming Ages

In great art galleries, such as the Metropolitan Museum of Art in New York City, you will find collections of famous portraits. The men and women depicted on canvas lived long ago, when they were no doubt very important or at least beloved. But today, when crowds pass by, admiring their portraits, it is not the men and women depicted who garner the praise, but the artists who painted them. That is what we admire—the skill, genius, and passion of the painter, which endures long after the subjects are no longer remembered.

We can draw an analogy to God's work in our salvation. God saved us and is doing his powerful work of transformation in our lives, so that in eternity to come his handiwork might be displayed in glory.

This is true in the present. People see the change that has come over us through our faith in Christ, and by our good works God is praised. But it is especially in the ages to come that God will be glorified through our salvation. Imagine the conversation of angels, millions of years from now, at the sight of a redeemed sinner resplendent in heavenly glory. "Is that not one of those rebels," the angels will marvel, "a son of Adam, corrupted by sin, guilty of the gravest offenses to God's honor and rule? But look at him, now that God has finished his salvation! He is radiant in the righteous robes of Christ, beautiful in the holiness that has been perfected by God's Spirit, beloved of God the Father and one closest to his heart, his own child and heir of glory!"

It is especially in the future ages that we will praise God for the blessings that have now only begun but that then will be in full bloom. Yet even with the burdens of this present sinful world, with the pains and degradation of a mortal body, with the torments and struggles of contending with sin, we still have ample reason to praise and thank God. And in the age to come, with glorified bodies, with a nature that is cleansed from every residue of evil, with a routine joy that far exceeds the best we ever attain in this present life, with what intensity and fervor will our voices give praise to God in heaven! We will be like Moses, who on the one side of the Red Sea, with Pharaoh's army bearing down, trembled and feared even though he trusted God, but who, once he had passed through the parted waters, had seen the destruction of Pharaoh's host, and was safe and secure on the other side, sang with unrestrained joy of the glory of Almighty God. In heaven, we will sing Moses' hymn: "The LORD is my strength and my song, and he has become my salvation; this is my God, and I will praise him" (Ex. 15:2).

In our present lives we are often afflicted, we stumble in sin, and the best of us are not very impressive when it comes to holiness and faith. It may be hard to believe, but everyone who is now joined to Christ in faith will one day be perfect in holiness and resplendent in the reflected glory of God. What an encouragement it is now to know what we will be then. Hugh Martin asks, "Does not this constrain my wonder, joy, surprise, and praise . . . that I should be called not only to receive freely an infinite, sovereign, undeserved love, but that my reception of it should be the means of throwing light, to the angelic beings, during the eternal ages, on the glorious character and perfections of God?"[4]

This is the very thing that God has promised in his Word: "Those who are wise shall shine like the brightness of the sky above; and those who turn many to righteousness, like the stars forever and ever" (Dan. 12:3). Paul writes in Romans 8:18, "I consider that the sufferings of this present time are not worth comparing with the glory that is to be revealed to us."

Therefore, however much we struggle in this pilgrim journey to heaven, those who walk with God are destined to display his glory forever, to the eternal praise of his name.

The Immeasurable Riches of Christ

I have defined God's glory as the revealing of the perfections of his attributes. But Paul has something specific about God in mind when it comes to our salvation, namely, that it glorifies "the immeasurable riches of his grace." In creation, God displayed the glory of his power, wisdom, and beauty. But if his grace were to be displayed in glory, then God needed to exercise grace toward us. God glorifies his attributes by exercising them. He glorifies his sovereignty by reigning, he glorifies his justice by judging, and he glorifies his grace by saving undeserving sinners like us.

This helps us to go at least partway in answering why God allowed sin to happen in the first place. God is not the author of sin (see 1 John 1:5), but since God is omnipotent and sovereign over all things (Rom. 11:36), the entry of sin was necessarily in accordance with his eternal decree. The question is: Why? Paul gives one answer in Romans 11:32: "For God has consigned all to disobedience, that he may have mercy on all." Our verse gives us another clue, that God ordained our salvation from sin to display the "immeasurable riches of his grace."

Donald Grey Barnhouse analogizes by telling of a store window he once saw in Paris. The shop was world-famous for making the finest, most delicate, most intricate white lace in all the world. Some of the best specimens were on display in the store window, laid out on a background of the blackest velvet. Looking at the display, Barnhouse thought of how God uses the dark background of sin to display the marvels and intricacies and riches of his grace, about which we would otherwise never have any idea.[5] John

Owen concurs, explaining that our redemption from sin simultaneously increases the blessing to God's elect while magnifying his glory to a greater extent than did even the creation of the world:

> God's purpose was to raise sinners to an inconceivably better condition than they were in before sin entered the world. God now appears more glorious than ever he did before. Now he is seen to be a God who pardons iniquity and sin and who is infinitely rich in grace. . . . To save sinners through believing will be seen to be a far more wonderful work than to create the world out of nothing.[6]

Paul writes that God glorifies "the immeasurable riches of his grace" through our salvation. What are these riches? To remind ourselves, we need only walk back through this letter to the Ephesians. In chapter 1, verse 3, Paul says that God "blessed us in Christ with every spiritual blessing," and then he goes on to tell us what they are. Verse 4 informs us that we were chosen by God before the foundation of the world to be holy in his sight. What is the value of that? What is it worth to be elected by God to receive the holiness without which you cannot get to heaven? According to verse 5, God predestined us to be adopted as his own sons in Christ. Verse 7 speaks of Christ's blood, shed for our forgiveness. Verse 9 speaks of the knowledge of the mystery of God's will, granted us through his Word. What do you possess that you would not give for these things?

When a jeweler wants to appraise a stone, he puts a special lens before his eye. Likewise, the riches of God's grace are seen only through the lens of faith. It is God's Word that reveals them to us, and faith in God's Word that makes these riches real to our lives.

If we have this faith and thereby see these riches, how can we be discontented in this present life? You say, "But I am poor in this world." Yes, but this life is short, and you will soon have eternal riches beyond counting! "But I am afflicted with temptations." Yes, but those temptations will have less effect on you as you grow in grace, and in eternity you will be spotless and pure, untouched by any sin. "But I am lonely." Yes, but you can have fellowship even now with the God of the universe, whose fatherly love is set upon you forever. "I am sick." Yes, and hard though that is, what is mortal will soon be clothed in immortality, and what is corruptible with the incorruptible. So even through tears—and all of us will shed them—Christians can have joy because of the immeasurable riches of God's grace.

One of my favorite Bible stories comes from the life of the prophet Jeremiah. The city of Jerusalem was besieged by the Babylonian army, and all the surrounding area had been trampled by enemy boots. God came to Jeremiah and told him to take his money and buy a plot of land in his hometown of Anathoth, which at that moment was occupied by the Babylonians. Jeremiah obeyed, buying land that no one else wanted, because to the eyes of sight it had no worth at all. By faith, Jeremiah saw the future promised by God. He knew that the town would be rebuilt and would prosper in the hand of the Lord. He was buying low, and later he would sell high when God's promises were fulfilled (see Jer. 32).

The same is true for us today. When it comes to eternity, Christians are the ultimate inside traders. We know exactly where to put our money and which investments are certain to take off in the light of glory! Jesus said that the kingdom of God is like a treasure that a man found hidden in a field. The man who found it "in his joy" went and sold all that he had and bought that field (Matt. 13:44). It is faith that enables us to see "the immeasurable riches of [God's] grace." If you are wise, then, instead of investing in this present evil, passing world, you will invest your hopes, your time, your money, your sweat and tears and prayers in the kingdom of God, where, like Jeremiah's field, the riches of God's grace will yield dividends for an eternity in glory.

The riches of God's grace are revealed in his "kindness toward us in Christ Jesus." What is the value to God of the grace by which we are saved, but the price of his own beloved Son? What was the cost of this grace to Jesus Christ? Though he was the eternal, divine, and glorious Son of God, he set aside his glory to be born in poverty and undertake all the troubles of life in this world. He suffered the scorn and abuse of men and endured the terror of God's holy wrath on the cross, all to deliver into our hands this grace of God that truly is immeasurable in worth. This is the grace given to us to be shown in eternity, and only eternity will be big enough for the full display of the infinite riches of God's grace for us in Christ.

To God Be the Glory

I began by saying that people today lack a sense of purpose or meaning. But Christians have been saved to a great purpose, for which we now live. The purpose of our salvation is not to take all our troubles away, but to give us the opportunity, in the midst of so many and great trials, to glorify God in this world. Jesus said, "You are the light of the world. . . . Let your light shine before others, so that they may see your good works and give glory to your Father who is in heaven" (Matt. 5:14–16). Just as our eyes cannot bear to stare into the sun, but can stand only to see its glorious rays reflected onto the nearby clouds, unbelievers whose sinful natures recoil from contemplating God may look at the reality of his grace in our lives and discover God's glory for themselves.

So how do we glorify God? We glorify God, as Jesus said, by doing good works in his name. We glorify God by telling others about his love and the free salvation that comes through faith in Christ. But most of all we glorify God through the holiness that he desires in us, by cultivating the fruit of his Spirit in our hearts, by being no longer conformed to the world but transformed by the renewing of our minds through his Word. God made us to bear his own image, and it is by the holiness that conforms to the character of Christ that we most glorify him in this world. Whatever else is different about individual Christians—and we are all very different in many ways—we are unified in this great purpose: to live for the glory of God in the beauty of holiness.

But I want to go even further and say that glorifying God is not only our purpose, but the great privilege of our lives. If you have ever met veterans of World War II, a war in which the issues of good and evil were clear and our soldiers knew themselves to be part of a noble crusade, you will find that they considered it the great privilege of their lives. Despite all the hardships they endured, some of them wounded and even bearing lifelong disabilities, they still say, "I am so honored to have been a part of it. And it was such a glory to be among such a great group of guys, a band of brothers and heroes!" That is how we should feel about our calling in Christ to bring glory to God. Martyn Lloyd-Jones writes:

> The privilege of being used of God in this way to vindicate His own eternal, glorious character! Why am I in this? Why did He ever look upon me? . . . Do we not all feel like saying that? Who am I, and what am I, that God should ever have looked upon me and chosen me to be part of His plan and His purpose . . . ? Christian people, think of yourselves like that, and go on to glory.[7]

Everyone—not just Christians, but everyone—will ultimately glorify God. Whether you are a believer or not, you will glorify God at the end of this age and forever after that. God's chief end is to glorify himself, and being all-powerful, God will certainly achieve that purpose in each of our lives. But there are other things to glorify about him besides his grace. God is just and holy, and he will glorify these attributes in the eternal condemnation of sinners who reject his gospel. James Montgomery Boice writes:

> Every person who has ever lived or will ever live must glorify God, either actively or passively, either willingly or unwillingly, either in heaven or in hell. You will glorify God. Either you will glorify him as the object of his mercy and glory, which will be seen in you. Or you will glorify him in your rebellion and unbelief by being made the object of his wrath and power at the final judgment.[8]

How much better for you to glorify God for his grace, exercised in his kindness to you in Jesus Christ, if you will turn from your sins, believe on the Lord Jesus Christ, and offer your life for the praise of the glory of the grace of our loving God.

Questions for Study and Reflection

1. How do Christians respond to the quest for significance that many people feel today?
2. What is God's ultimate purpose in salvation by grace alone? How does your answer shape your view of Christianity?
3. If self-glory is wrong for men and women, why is it proper for God? The author said, "The chief end of God is to glorify God." Do you agree with this? Comment on the significance of this statement.

4. How is the knowledge of our future inheritance in Christ an encouragement during the struggles and trials of today?
5. What are "the immeasurable riches of God's grace"? What did it cost God to give us these riches? What are they worth to us?
6. If we are saved to glorify God, how do we do this? How are you being challenged to live for God's glory?

7

By Grace, through Faith

Ephesians 2:8–9

For by grace you have been saved through faith. And this is not your own doing; it is the gift of God, not a result of works, so that no one may boast.
—Ephesians 2:8–9

Some verses in the Bible are so important to our understanding of the gospel that every Christian should know them by heart. John 3:16 is one of them: "For God so loved the world, that he gave his only Son, that whoever believes in him should not perish but have eternal life." Ephesians 2:8–9 falls into this same category, as Bible teaching essential to a sound grasp of Christianity. Here, the apostle Paul makes the definitive statement relating to grace, salvation, faith, and works: "For by grace you have been saved through faith. And this is not your own doing; it is the gift of God, not a result of works, so that no one may boast."

Salvation by Grace

In Ephesians 2:1–10, Paul's purpose is to explain how salvation comes to us as individuals. But he wants to do more than explain the doctrine of salvation: he wants to magnify the glory of God because of it. To that end, his key message is the one that opens verse 8: "For by grace you have been saved."

For Paul, the stupendous good news of the gospel is that God saves sinners by grace alone. Martyn Lloyd-Jones explains, "It is in spite of us that God forgives us. We are Christian not because we are good people; we are Christian because, though we were bad people, God had mercy upon us and sent his Son to die for us. We are saved entirely by the grace of God; there is no human contribution whatsoever, and if you think there is, you are denying the central biblical doctrine."[1] This is what Paul has been driving at since he began chapter 2 detailing mankind's depraved condition. Men and women in sin are spiritually dead, he has said, as unable to contribute something positive to their salvation as a dead man is unable to raise himself from the grave (Eph. 2:1–3). This is why Paul, when he begins explaining our salvation, in verses 4–6 breaks in and exclaims, "By grace you have been saved" (Eph. 2:5). This is why verse 7 gives as the reason for our salvation "so that in the coming ages he might show the immeasurable riches of his grace." Salvation is all of grace; this is the glory of Christianity, that God saves us who had no power to save ourselves, who had nothing to commend ourselves to God, and who had nothing to offer in payment. This is Paul's great explanation of salvation: "For by grace you have been saved" (Eph. 2:8).

We always need to define our terms, and there are two main ways in which the word *grace* may be taken. First, it denotes *an attitude within God.* God is gracious. A. W. Tozer writes, "Grace is the good pleasure of God that inclines Him to bestow benefits upon the undeserving. . . . It is . . . a self-caused propensity to pity the wretched, spare the guilty, welcome the outcast, and bring into favor those who were before under just disapprobation."[2] As the result of God's grace, Christians receive blessings we have not deserved and could never merit.

It is grace that causes a wealthy man to voluntarily pay the tuition of a poor student who could otherwise never go to college. It is by grace that a family takes in an orphan and adopts him or her into a loving home. But all these human examples, glorious as they are, pale before the grace of God. God responds to the guilt and rebellion of his creatures by offering his own Son to pay the debt of their sin and by renewing them to love and serve him and enjoy blessings as his children. We are saved, then, because of the gracious love in God that causes him to show so much kindness to us in Jesus Christ.

No wonder that when Paul considers God's grace, he wants us to praise God. What a terrible pity that so many people hate and refuse God, not knowing his grace. This is what we need to tell people, that God has grace to forgive them and bless them. This is what God wants for people—to be their God and be gracious to them.

The second way in which we should consider the term *grace* is as *a system of disbursement.* God has blessings to give. God has eternal life to bestow on his creatures; he has fellowship with himself; he has glory in the blessed reign of his Son, Jesus Christ. The question is: How will God grant these blessings?

There really are only two ways in which we can gain or receive something: either by earning it or by receiving it as a gift. So it is with God. He may grant his blessings on the basis of merit or on the basis of grace. In Romans 4:4, Paul acknowledges these options: "Now to the one who works, his wages are not counted as a gift but as his due." These are the only two possibilities: as a gift or as our due. History shows that man prefers merit as the way of gaining God's blessings. This is what human religion always teaches unless corrected by the Bible. Man wants to stand on his own two feet and pay his own way. Man wants to preserve his own dignity, even in the presence of God, and receive a salvation that will promote his own glory.

The problem is that man has merited not blessing from God but condemnation. This was Paul's point in Ephesians 2:1–3: "By nature [we are] children of wrath." Just by being born as members of the rebel human race, just by being the offspring of the sinners Adam and Eve, no man or woman can ever stand before God and demand blessing. Furthermore, as Paul writes in Romans 3:23, "All have sinned and fall short of the glory of God." Yes, merit is a way in which you might procure God's blessings, but it is a way that is no longer open to you or any other sinner. The prophet Isaiah knew this, lamenting that even our supposed good works "are like a polluted garment" (Isa. 64:6), hopelessly tainted by sin.

People say, "All I want is for God to be just toward me." But you do not really want God's justice; under God's justice you will be justly condemned to hell. But because God is gracious, and because he wants his grace to be glorified forever, God offers another way for you to be saved: by grace. God satisfies his justice through the death of Jesus Christ in your place. God will then bless you with salvation—forgiveness and eternal life—as a gift. The result is, as verse 9 concludes, "that no one may boast" before God. God wants to be God and he wants the worship of his people, not the boasting of self-righteous creatures. "Humble yourselves before the Lord," the Bible instructs, "and he will exalt you" (James 4:10). God delights to save by grace, so that no one may boast before him.

SALVATION THROUGH FAITH

The Bible makes it plain that not everyone is or will be saved, so there has to be something that distinguishes those who have received God's grace and that brings grace to them. Some people think this is nationality; some Americans seem to think, for instance, that God must always bless America. Others think it is church membership or baptism; so long as they stay in the church and receive its approval, they will be all right. Others believe it is some intense emotional experience that ensures God's favor. But Paul tells us in verse 8 the one thing that provides us with God's grace and thus saves us: "For by grace you have been saved through faith." Salvation is *by grace* and *through faith.*

Faith is another word that requires definition. Norman Vincent Peale popularized a concept of faith that is widely held today. To him, faith was a general sort of optimism. His best-selling book was titled *The Power of Positive Thinking.* What we should do, he said, is just believe that all things are possible to us, and they will be. He wrote, "According to your faith in yourself, according to your faith in your job, according to your faith in God, this far will you get and no further."[3] Faith, according to this view, is a power that you need to exercise.

But this is not the Bible's teaching regarding faith. What matters about biblical faith is not the faith itself but faith's object. What matters is not just *that* you believe, but *what* you believe and *in whom* you believe. If what you believe in is not true and saving, then your faith will be in vain. Christian faith is in God and in Jesus Christ, in the truths of God's Word and his promises for those who believe. Faith is relying on God, receiving him and his Word for salvation. God has spoken, and we are to believe his Word; God has acted for our salvation, and we are to rely on his saving work in Jesus Christ.

When we think of saving faith, we should think of three necessary components. The first of these is *knowledge.* To have faith in something, you must have knowledge and understanding of it. This is why the Bible is so important to Christian faith. We must know what God has revealed about himself, what he says about us and our situation, what he has done for us, and especially about Jesus Christ and his life, death, and resurrection for our salvation.

But knowledge alone is not enough. Plenty of scholars can explain all the doctrines of the Bible, but do not believe they are true. Therefore, saving faith must include *belief* or *assent.* Not only must we know what God has revealed, but we must believe in it.

But even that is not enough to have saving faith. The apostle James pointed out that the demons know about God and believe that he is who he says he is. But they tremble! (James 2:19). Saving faith not only requires that we know and believe what the Bible says about God and Jesus Christ, but also requires *commitment.*

The first part of commitment is *trust.* Committing to God means trusting in him and in his Word and in the Savior, Jesus Christ. Trust involves personal acceptance and reliance. The Westminster Confession of Faith helpfully states that "the principal acts of saving faith are accepting, receiving, and resting upon Christ alone for justification, sanctification, and eternal life" (14.2). Charles Spurgeon writes, "The chief part of faith lies in . . . taking hold of it as being ours, and in the resting on it for salvation. . . . It will not save me to know that Christ is *a* Saviour; but it will save me to *trust* him to be *my Saviour.*"[4]

Commitment also involves a *surrender* of ourselves to God. Arthur Pink explains that faith

> lies in the complete surrender of the heart and life to a divine Person. It consists in a throwing down of the

> weapons of our rebellion against Him. It is the total disowning of allegiance to the old master—Satan, sin, self, and a declaring "we *will* have this Man to reign over us" (Lk. 19:14). . . . It is "receiving Christ Jesus *the Lord*" (Col. 2:6), giving Him the throne of our hearts, turning over to Him the control and regulation of our lives.[5]

This is precisely what we find in the Bible when people come to saving faith in Jesus Christ. Doubting Thomas knew Jesus, but he held back from believing. Jesus appeared to him after the resurrection and offered to have Thomas place his fingers in his wounds. At that moment, Thomas came to a saving faith: he worshiped Jesus, saying, "My Lord and my God!" (John 20:28).

Zacchaeus was a sinful tax collector who preyed on the weak. When Jesus passed through Jericho, Zacchaeus climbed into a sycamore tree to see him. Jesus called Zacchaeus to himself, and we know from what happened that Zacchaeus committed himself to Jesus in saving faith. He replied, "Lord, the half of my goods I give to the poor. And if I have defrauded anyone of anything, I restore it fourfold" (Luke 19:8).

Acts 16 tells us about Lydia, a successful businesswoman whom Paul met in Philippi. God opened her heart, and having believed, she opened up her house and urged that Paul allow her to support him and the work of the church. Believing, she gave herself wholly to Christ.

The apostle Paul himself provides a prime example of saving faith. We are introduced to him as a violent hater of Christians, devoting himself to their torment and destruction. But when Jesus revealed himself to Paul and called him into his service, Paul offered the whole of his life to proclaiming the gospel. He who had wielded a harsh sword of hatred became the greatest teacher of the glory of God's grace. His name had previously been Saul of Tarsus, but to mark this definitive change in his life, the Lord renamed him Paul, the apostle of grace.

These are examples of true saving faith, which always culminates in a commitment to Christ that involves personal trust and surrender. Saving faith involves what happens in a wedding ceremony. In the gospel, God's Son says to us, "I will be your Savior and will take you as my bride." In faith, we reply, "I trust in you alone for my salvation, and I give myself into your service and rely on you for all my blessing forever." Jesus then gives us his own name. We were Sinner but now are Christian, thus denoting the change that is to characterize our lives.

Faith is a subject that is often confused, which is why we need such careful teaching on it. We have already noted that faith is not merely a sort of optimism, but depends on its object. Furthermore, saving faith involves knowledge, belief, and commitment. But Paul says three things in verses 8–9 that we also need to appreciate.

Faith the Conduit of Grace

The first statement has to do with the word *through,* which Paul applies to faith. We are saved by grace and *through* faith. The point is how faith functions in our salvation. Paul teaches that grace comes to us *through* faith. Faith is the vessel in which grace is received. Think of a picnic on a hot day. A large container of soothing lemonade is available, but you still need a cup into which to pour it. Without a cup, you cannot have anything to drink. The cup is not a way of earning the lemonade, but is the means of receiving it. Likewise, faith does not merit us God's grace, but is the means whereby we receive salvation from God.[6]

Perhaps an even better way of understanding how we are saved through faith is to think of faith as the channel by which salvation flows to us. Grace flows through faith as water flows through a pipe. This keeps us from thinking that the strength or virtue of our faith saves us; in fact, we are saved by the grace that comes through our faith. Salvation is *by grace*—that is the substance of our salvation—and *through faith*—that is the channel by which salvation comes to us.

THE GIFT OF GOD

Second, we must understand where faith comes from. Do you trust Christ because you are better or more spiritually motivated than people who don't? Is faith just the way in which we prove our worth and earn salvation? Many people in the church think this way, that faith is basically a work that God accepts because full obedience to the law is too hard. Yet Paul destroys such a theory in verse 8: "This is not your own doing; it is the gift of God."

Scholars dispute what Paul is saying here. Does "gift" point back to "saved" or to "faith"? Is Paul saying that salvation is not our own doing or that faith is not our own doing, but is the gift of God? The answer is that it does not matter; Paul's point is the same in either case. If salvation is not of our own doing, and salvation comes through faith, then Paul's point must be that faith is God's gift and not something that we produce or possess on our own.

This is why the salvation that comes through faith is by grace alone. Obviously, exercising faith is something we do; we are actively involved in it. We have to believe and commit to God. But since faith is something that God works into us, something that he gives out of his own sheer grace, salvation is not a result of our works. In Romans 4:16, Paul writes, "That is why it depends on faith, in order that the promise may rest on grace." Faith is the one way in which I may be personally entered into salvation, in such a way that salvation remains the gift of God's grace, with all glory going to him. Faith is not what we contribute to God, but what God contributes to us by the power of his Holy Spirit. God made this promise in Ezekiel 36:26: "I will give you a new heart, and a new spirit I will put within you. And I will remove the heart of stone from your flesh and give you a heart of flesh."

Why is it that you believe on Jesus, whereas your old friend does not? Both of you were, according to Paul, "dead in [your] trespasses." So why are you saved and not others? The answer is not because of something you did or something better in you, for there is nothing better in you. The answer is the free and sovereign grace of God, who gives faith to those whom he would save, through which we receive Jesus Christ and all the blessings that are in him.

For this reason, we should never trust in our faith—weak and inconstant as it is—but in God himself, who showed his grace to us by giving us the faith that joins us to a strong Savior.

Not by Works

Paul makes this teaching clear with the third statement he makes regarding faith. First he described it as the vessel or channel through which grace comes to us. Then he called faith God's gift. Finally, he contrasts faith with works: "By grace you have been saved through faith . . . , not a result of works, so that no one may boast" (Eph. 2:8–9).

We contrasted grace with merit. Those are the two ways of salvation—and, having sinned, we now can be saved only by grace. Similarly, faith and works are two opposing instruments of salvation. We do not merit salvation through works, but we receive grace through faith.

Another way of saying this is to observe that you must trust either in your own works or in the works of Jesus Christ.

Someone's works must commend you to God, causing him to receive you as worthy and righteous. Most people today are trusting in their own works. "Why should you be allowed to enter into heaven?" we ask. They reply in terms of their own works: "I am a basically good person, I have attended church, I have given money, I have prayed, I have memorized verses in the Bible, I have not committed any serious crimes."

That is salvation through works! How appealing it is according to the spirit of our age. Self-justification is the way of man. Self-glory is the kind of salvation that sinners want. But understand that God utterly rejects anyone who tries to come to him that way. Whatever you think of yourself, God cannot and will not get over the reality of your sin. You have exalted yourself over him and stained yourself with iniquity. "The wages of sin is death," he declares (Rom. 6:23). Jesus says to such people that unless they rely on his saving work, "you will die in your sins" (John 8:24).

This was all dramatized at the beginning of the Bible when Cain and Abel, the two sons of Adam and Eve, sought acceptance with God. Cain offered his works, the fruit of the soil he had farmed. It seemed so impressive to him, but not to God. Abel came not with a symbol of his works but with a symbol of his faith in God's promise to save. He brought a lamb, pointing forward to the cross of Jesus Christ. Cain by works was rejected, while Abel through faith was blessed.

Abel put his faith not in his own works but in the work of the promised Savior. So must we. Christians are saved by works—but they are not works that we do. We are saved by the work of Christ, fulfilling all righteousness in our place and dying for our sins on the cross. By faith, we repudiate our own works and receive his for salvation. As Augustus Toplady wrote: "Not the labors of my hands can fulfil thy law's demands; / could my zeal no respite know, could my tears forever flow, / all for sin could not atone; thou must save, and thou alone."[7]

"The wages of sin is death," Paul warned. That is our problem, and our works cannot solve it. He therefore gave the solution: "But the free gift of God is eternal life in Christ Jesus our Lord" (Rom. 6:23). For this reason, salvation by grace alone, through faith alone, is salvation in Jesus Christ alone. It is coming to God as Abel did, looking in faith to the cross of Christ, where the grace of God brought forth a Savior to take away our sin and grant us eternal life.

No Boasting?

Paul concludes this vital passage by saying "so that no one may boast." I want to conclude this chapter by saying that Paul really does not mean what he seems to say. Paul does not mean that in response to this salvation by grace, through faith in Christ, we ought not to boast. What he means is that we must not boast in ourselves. But the very thing Paul wants is for us to boast in God, to glory in God, to extol before all the world this salvation that is by grace, through faith in Jesus Christ.

Indeed, this is the best way for you and me to make a difference in our generation. Ours is an age that delights in boasting in self. Ours is the time of the end-zone dance and the self-promoting political ad. Christians are to stand in contrast to the vain boasts of a spiritually dead, sin-enslaved, God-condemned world, by living humbly before God. By grace, we speak of a God whose mercy overwhelms our sin. Through faith, we bear testimony to an all-sufficient salvation freely given from the hands of our loving God. And this is our boast, given by the testimony of our lives: "To God alone be the glory, for the riches of his grace and his kindness toward us in Christ Jesus."

Questions for Study and Reflection

1. The author states that "for Paul, the stupendous good news of the gospel is that God saves sinners by grace alone." How would you explain to a non-Christian that salvation is by grace alone?
2. Romans 4:4 outlines two ways one might gain blessings. What are these two ways? Which way does unregenerate man always prefer? Which way does God save sinners?
3. Paul says that salvation is by grace and through faith. How would you explain faith to a non-Christian? What does it mean that we are saved "through" faith?
4. How does a wedding ceremony typify salvation through faith? What does the author mean by saying that faith requires surrendering to Christ?
5. If faith is God's gift, how can God require us to believe? What does it mean to say that salvation and faith are God's gifts? How does God give faith?

8

God's Workmanship

Ephesians 2:10

For we are his workmanship, created in Christ Jesus for good works, which God prepared beforehand, that we should walk in them.
—Ephesians 2:10

One of the issues of greatest confusion and controversy in Christian theology is the place of works in our salvation. Despite the clear Bible teaching on this matter, many Christians err on one side or the other.

One error is to make works a condition of salvation. This is the error of the Roman Catholic Church, which teaches that we must be justified by a combination of faith and works. Their formula is faith + works = justification. Roman Catholics teach that faith is like the band of a ring, and works are like the jewel it holds and that gives it value. The whole purpose of faith, therefore, is to present works for salvation.

The Protestant Reformation made its principal quarrel with Rome over this very issue. The problem with salvation by faith and works is that you can never have peace. You can never know that you are saved because you never know that your works are enough. Indeed, according to the apostle Paul, your works can never be good enough to justify you. "No one does good," he insists, "not even one" (Rom. 3:12, quoting Ps. 14:3). Therefore, he taught in Ephesians 2:8–9, "By grace you have been saved through faith . . . , not a result of works." Faith is the ring, we insist, that presents not our works but the jewel of Christ and his work for us.

The error on the other side of works is held by many evangelicals. This error says that since salvation is not by works, then works don't matter at all. So long as I believe on Jesus, so long as I once made a decision for Christ or walked down an aisle at the minister's invitation, then whatever else I do has no impact on my salvation. This is called the *antinomian* view, *nomos* being the word for "law" and *anti* meaning "opposed to."

In recent years, some have insisted that so long as you profess faith in Jesus Christ, your salvation is assured even if you never bear any spiritual fruit and if you continue in a lifestyle of sin all the rest of your life.[1] Nothing could be more in conflict with the Bible's teaching. As Paul asked in Romans 6:1–2, "Are we to continue in sin that grace may abound? By no means! How can we who died to sin still live in it?" I fear that many who hold to such a view, while filling our churches, will hear at the end of their lives the dreadful words from our Lord: "I never knew you; depart from me, you workers of lawlessness" (Matt. 7:23), that is, literally, "you antinomians"!

The Necessity of Works

The first thing Ephesians 2:10 teaches us, then, is the necessity of good works. Works do not cause salvation, but salvation necessarily causes good works. Having been saved from sin by grace through faith, we are saved to a life of good works as part of the ongoing process of growth in grace and holiness that we call sanctification. "For we are [God's] workmanship, created in Christ Jesus for good works, which God prepared beforehand, that we should walk in them."

Charles Spurgeon points out that if we were to auction off the pieces of salvation, the bidding for forgiveness would go very high but few would offer much for holiness. He writes, "Suppose I took sanctification, the giving up of all sin, a thorough change of heart, leaving off drunkenness and swearing; many would say, 'I don't want that; I should like to go to heaven, but I do not want that holiness." But God is not auctioning off mere portions of salvation; you must have all or none. You must have Christ as Savior and Lord or not at all. Spurgeon concludes, "God will never divide the gospel. He will not give justification to that man, and sanctification to another—pardon to one, and holiness to another. No, it all goes together. Whom he calls, them he justifies; whom he justifies, them he sanctifies" (Rom. 8:30).[2]

Just as light and heat are inseparably joined to the rays of the sun, likewise justification and sanctification, forgiveness and a life transformed to do good works, are inseparable parts of the gospel. We are saved by faith alone, but saving faith never is alone. It always produces the good works that God desires.

This is Paul's teaching all through his many letters. In Titus 2:14 he writes that Jesus died "to redeem us from all lawlessness and to purify for himself a people for his own possession who are zealous for good works." In 2 Corinthians 9:8, he teaches that God provides for all our needs, "so that . . . you may abound in every good work."

It is especially Jesus' teaching that we think of when it comes to the need for good works. In John 15:8, he taught, "By this my Father is glorified, that you bear much fruit and so prove to be my disciples." The fruit of good works does not make us disciples, but it glorifies God and proves that we are Christ's followers.

All of this shows that good works are necessary to salvation, necessary not as a *condition* or as a *cause* but as a *consequence*. Without good works there is no reason to believe you are a disciple of Christ, and there is much reason to doubt that you are. "By this we may know that we are in [Christ]: whoever says he abides in him ought to walk in the same way in which he walked" (1 John 2:5–6).

A good way to assess your spiritual state is how you respond to teaching such as this. Do you resent being told that salvation involves good works and a changed life? Would you prefer a salvation that delivered you from the penalty of sin but not from sin itself? What is your attitude toward holiness? Do you want a purer, more godly, more loving heart, or are you happy with the one you have? The salvation that Jesus gives is one that involves a desire for a transformed life, and an increasing realization of that desire.

The Source of Works

Whenever the Bible talks about the necessity of good works, people begin to get nervous and uncertain about themselves. That is because Christians know all too well the power of our sin. But Paul reminds us in Ephesians 2:10 not only of the necessity of good works but also of their source: "We are [God's] workmanship, created in Christ Jesus for good works." This means that the source of our good works is God's own work in us. We are saved by grace and grace is also the cause of our growth in holiness, so that our sanctification and works do not rely on our strength but on God's.

Earlier in this chapter, Paul said that God came to us when we were spiritually dead, when we had neither the slightest desire to serve him nor the smallest bit of spiritual life. Paul described our salvation as a spiritual resurrection (Eph. 2:4–5). It was God who breathed spiritual life into our hearts in the first place, and it is God who will continue to supply us with the strength we need to bear the fruit of good deeds.

I find that many Christians lack hope for godliness and strength for leading a changed life because they think they must do so in their own power. But Paul says that we are God's workmanship. Therefore, it is his work in us that will change us. I think the best statement of this truth is found in Philippians 2:12–13. Paul writes, "Work out your own salvation with fear and trembling." That statement means that we are to apply our faith to every area of our lives, changing our approach to work, play, the way we treat people, sexuality, money, career ambitions, life goals, and daily habits. But lest we despair of so difficult a task, Paul adds, "For it is God who works in you, both to will and to work for his good pleasure." Yes, you have to work it out, but only as God is first working it into you. We change our approach because God himself changes our attitudes—changing our minds, hearts, and desires to match his own.

This transformation takes place especially through God's provision of the ordinary means of grace: God's Word, prayer, and the sacraments. It is impossible to overstate the importance of coming to church each week, worshiping God, and hearing his Word faithfully taught. The same is true about personal Bible study and prayer. Paul writes in 2 Timothy 3:16–17, "All Scripture is breathed out by God and profitable for teaching, for reproof, for correction, and for training in righteousness, that the man of God may be competent, equipped for every good work."

Paul specifies that we were created for good works "in Christ Jesus." If you are born again and have a living faith, it is so that you will become more and more like Jesus, and so that Jesus himself will work in you powerfully through the Holy Spirit he sends.

This is what transforms our Christianity from a weak defeatism to a mighty boldness to do God's will. How can I dare to shine brightly for God? Because I was created anew in Christ for this very purpose, and it is God's work in me to do this very thing! How can I ever leave behind former sins? Because God is giving me new pleasures that rise far above the old. How can I gain power to break deeply ingrained habits and even addictions? Through the power God supplies in answer to prayers. How can I be willing to sacrifice for others and stop living for myself? Because I know a power working in me, a heavenly spring of life from which I am now able to drink, the cup of faith having been placed into my hand by God himself. This powerful grace is not worked into me at random, but as I devote myself to God's Word, prayer, and sacred worship in God's church.

This is why I have been greatly distressed by a recent Christian fad of wearing clothing and jewelry with the initials *WWJD*. This stands for "What Would Jesus Do?" There are two problems with this approach. The first is that much of what Jesus did was performed in his unique office of Messiah, a burden and calling that we do not share. Moreover, the WWJD approach assumes that Jesus supplies only an example, leaving us to supply our own power. Instead of asking what Jesus *would do* if he were in our situation, we do better to ask, "What *will* Jesus do as I trust him, as I call on him for strength, as I renew my mind and heart through his Word?" Christianity is not a human effort to imitate an absent Christ. Rather, it is

"Christ in you, the hope of glory" (Col. 1:27), or, as Paul says elsewhere, "It is no longer I who live, but Christ who lives in me" (Gal. 2:20).

Jesus is not like a mountain guide who merely climbs up before us, shows us the way, and then calls down for us to follow. Instead, he lets down a strong rope—which we might compare to his Holy Spirit—and for every feeble step we take upward he pulls mightily on that rope, so that far sooner than we imagine we have climbed far higher than we ever thought we would. God's present working in Christ, by the Spirit, through the ordinary means of grace, is the source of the new and glorious life we begin to lead as his cherished people.

A Plan for Works

The third thing Paul tells us in Ephesians 2:10 is the most amazing of all. He writes of the necessity of works, and the source of works, and then goes so far as to speak of a plan for works that God has for each of our lives.

Some time ago I saw a humorous bumper sticker to this effect: "God sent me into this world with work that I was to do. I'm so far behind that I will never die!" According to the apostle Paul, the first part of that bumper sticker's saying is most certainly true: God has assigned us work to do. He describes our good works as those "which God prepared beforehand, that we should walk in them."

The idea is that God's plan for each of us includes specific good works that he has foreordained for us to do. This does not mean merely that God has designed that we would do good works in general. The Greek word means not merely "to intend" but "to prepare in advance." Not only were we created for good works, but good works were created for us. Our job, Paul says, is to "walk in them." God has laid down a path of situations and good works for us, and we are to walk down that path, seeking to do his will.

What good works has God ordained? First, God has revealed his moral will in the law. Believers need to know and study the Ten Commandments; we will find that they provide us a path of life. According to David, "The precepts of the LORD are right, rejoicing the heart; the commandment of the LORD is pure, enlightening the eyes" (Ps. 19:8).

In every situation we enter, we are to obey God's law—worshiping him only, renouncing all idols, reverencing God's name, keeping the Sabbath holy, honoring those in authority, not doing violence but promoting others' well-being, guarding against lust, respecting others' property, speaking the truth in love, and cultivating godliness with contentment. The Ten Commandments are enormously practical. The shame is that so few believers even know what they are, much less use them as a guide for good works. As you go to work, as you start a day at school or in the home, you should say to God, "I have stored up your word in my heart, that I might not sin against you" (Ps. 119:11).

Second, God has given each of us particular gifts, abilities, and opportunities. We are to be faithful stewards of them, serving God's kingdom, promoting God's glory, and imparting practical blessings. Some of us have the gift of teaching, so we are to teach. Others are empowered for exhortation and encouragement; others are gifted in helps, or in administration, or in comfort. Each of us is given a role to play and a way to serve, and it is important that we do our part as God predestined for us to do.

I find that a common problem in life is envy and discontentment. Everyone wants to be in someone else's situation. People in the north dream of Florida; Southerners dream of snow. Likewise, many Christians want the gifts that somebody else has, especially if they lead to praise and notoriety.

But you are where you are and who you are because God wanted you to be this way. He has good to be done in your life that no one else can do. He wants your life to provide a particular lens on his glory that none other can. You just have to be yourself in Christ, and do the good works that God prepared in advance for you to do.

Third, there are good works that all Christians are to embrace as a willing duty. We are all different in many ways, but we are all called to pray, spread the gospel, worship with God's people, and support God's work through generous giving. This is God's plan for us, and he has made full provision for our blessing through obedience.

If we will take just these three categories seriously—obeying God's law, using our gifts, fulfilling the duties that all Christians share—our lives will be utterly transformed to the praise of God. We and others will see what Paul was so excited about in the teaching of this chapter. He began chapter 2 by describing a life, a walk, under the power of the world, the devil, and the flesh. But now we walk in the power of God, leading a life that is energized by grace and godliness. What an exciting change!

One conclusion to be drawn is that your life matters. There are things you can do that nobody else can do. Although you do not know what lies around the next corner, you know that, whatever it is, you can do God's will in it because God created it for you and you for it. G. Campbell Morgan wrote:

> If I can once accept this teaching and rest upon it I shall take my way into every new circumstance knowing these two things absolutely: first, God has prepared me in Christ Jesus for whatever the day has in store for me, and, secondly, all that to which I come, step by step as the veil recedes or the mists melt, though unknown to me, is not unknown to Him. Good works are afore

> prepared, afore ordained for us that we should walk in them.[3]

Then, when it comes time for you to die, you can have the satisfaction of knowing that all your work is done.

In the spring of 2000, the famous Bible teacher James Montgomery Boice learned that he had only weeks to live because of an aggressive cancer. He began working furiously, harnessing his rapidly fading strength to finish important projects and order the affairs of his far-flung ministries. Before he got very far, however, it became clear that he would never get it done. Was he frustrated? Angry? I will never forget the peace and the satisfied joy on his face when he said to me, "My work is now finished. I have done all I can, and therefore all that God intended for me to do in this life is complete." Not able to tie up all the loose ends, he simply put them into God's hand. He then experienced what the voice from heaven stated in the book of Revelation, "Blessed are the dead who die in the Lord. . . . They [will] rest from their labors, for their deeds follow them!" (Rev. 14:13).

God's Workmanship

In the great words that begin verse 10, Paul sums up all that he has been teaching about salvation: "We are his workmanship." The Greek word is *poiēma,* from which comes our word *poem.* It is a general term for a work of art. This means that our salvation is God's work and relies on his almighty power and sovereign will. It also means that out of all God's great creations, the redeemed sinner who believes and lives for God is the greatest of all his masterworks.

"The heavens declare the glory of God," observes Psalm 19:1. Look out at night and see the splashing of lights from distant galaxies, and you know something of the grandeur of God's creation. Yet as marvelous as all that is, the cosmos is not God's masterwork. Find the most perfect shoreline. Watch as the sunset dances on the waters. Or stand beneath the purple mountains bathed in snow, pillars of granite thrusting skyward. The beauty of nature is overwhelming, and yet these things are not God's highest work of art.

Psalm 8 reminds us that the tiny cry of a baby displays the glory of God. Surely this is the apex of the natural creation, a newborn baby, so complex and yet simple, eyes open, arms reaching for life. It is a physical marvel, its mind a dazzling computer recording everything it experiences. Its eyes focus light on the retina, simultaneously stimulating 125 million nerve endings. In a millisecond, that data is processed by the brain into a single image.[4] What a display of God's wisdom and power!

But there is something even more magnificent than that, proclaims our verse. God's highest masterpiece is the man or woman long dead in sin, whom God raised from spiritual death, and who is now saved to do good works in his name. God is spirit, and here is the great marvel of the spiritual realm, where Christ is enthroned. "If anyone is in Christ," Paul wrote, "he is a new creation. The old has passed away; behold, the new has come" (2 Cor. 5:17). That is God's masterwork of art, accomplished by the blood of Christ and the breath of the Holy Spirit.

This is the work taking place in your life now, if you are in Christ. It means that whatever God is calling you to do, he will ensure that you are able to do it. Knowing this, Paul declares, "I can do all things through him who strengthens me" (Phil. 4:13). It means that whatever trials or sufferings you are enduring, they have a purpose in God's plan for your life. You are his workmanship, and he is equipping you for good works to come. It means that what really matters is not where you are in God's plan for your life, but that you are in Christ, that you are born again, and that you are therefore an in-progress masterpiece of God's grace. And what God has begun by grace, he will complete and perfect in glory.

Let me conclude with just a few questions. Do you have experience with what Paul is saying here? Are you aware of the gentle but unrelenting pressure of God's loving hands on the clay of your life? Do you desire for more of God, more of his Word, more of his Spirit? Do you yearn for holiness? Are you doing works you never thought you would do, acting in ways that can be accounted for only by God?

If you know nothing of these things, it is a warning that things are not well with your soul. Especially if you want only to be forgiven but not to be changed, then you completely misunderstand the salvation that God is offering you. Martyn Lloyd-Jones rightly asserts: "There is no value in a profession of Christianity unless it is accompanied by a desire to be like Christ, a desire to be rid of sin, a desire after positive holiness."[5]

Until this has happened to you, then put aside all thought of works—because you cannot do them. What you need is to be born again, to be saved by grace through faith. But if you already have the desire not only to be forgiven but to be changed, to be rid of sin, and to be holy, then take heart. Rejoice! For that can only be because you are in Christ and God is working into you what he wants you to start working out. Press on to do good works in his power and to the glory of his name. "For we are his workmanship, created in Christ Jesus for good works, which God prepared beforehand, that we should walk in them."

Questions for Study and Reflection

1. What are the two ways in which Christians err in their thinking about works and salvation? What is antinomianism? Do you have any experience with Christians or churches that do not emphasize obedience or holiness? What was the experience like?

2. In what sense are good works *necessary* to salvation? What is the difference between works being necessary as a *consequence*, versus as a *condition* of salvation?
3. Is it possible for Christians to possess the "parts" of salvation that they like? What does it say about us that we would prefer some parts of salvation but not others? How should we pray in response to this situation?
4. What is the relationship between a believer's good works and God's grace? How is it said that God is the source of our good works? What does the author mean by "the ordinary means of grace," and how do they strengthen a believer's faith?
5. Discuss the author's statement "Christianity is not a human effort to imitate an absent Christ." How is this so? What expression might we put in its place?
6. Does God have a plan for our good works? How does this work out in practice? How does an awareness of God's plan for our good works shape our prayer life?
7. Is it accurate to say that believers are God's *poem*? In what sense is this meant? What then is the purpose and the goal of our life?

9

Without Christ

Ephesians 2:11–12

Therefore remember that at one time you Gentiles in the flesh, called "the uncircumcision" by what is called the circumcision, which is made in the flesh by hands—remember that you were at that time separated from Christ, alienated from the commonwealth of Israel and strangers to the covenants of promise, having no hope and without God in the world.
—Ephesians 2:11–12

"Remember!" That has been the rallying cry of many a statesman and orator. "Remember the Alamo!" was the motto that led Sam Houston's Texas Rangers in their war with Mexico. "Never Forget" is today emblazoned on T-shirts and bumper stickers over photographs of the World Trade Center towers and the numbers 9–11–01.

"Remember" is also one of the most important commands in the Bible. Our Lord Jesus, speaking from heaven to the churches in the book of Revelation, commanded, "Remember, then, what you received and heard. Keep it, and repent" (Rev. 3:3).

When Israel entered into the Promised Land, remembering was given to them as the key to future faithfulness. The people had just come through the exodus—a great deliverance from bondage into freedom. Moses warned them, "Take care, and keep your soul diligently, lest you forget the things that your eyes have seen, and lest they depart from your heart all the days of your life. Make them known to your children and your children's children" (Deut. 4:9). Remember! When the people failed to remember, as the book of Judges tells us, a generation grew up that fell into sin and judgment.

I know of a mother who sends her children out the door each morning, saying, "Remember who you are, and whose you are!" That is what Paul has to say to us. Having given some of the clearest and most glorious teaching about salvation in Ephesians 2:1–10, he commands us in the next verse, "Therefore remember!"

This is the very first command that Paul gives in Ephesians, which indicates its significance. Before he gets to any of the practical instruction that will follow, he first commands us, "Remember!" This is how the Christian life is lived, by remembering what God has done for us and living in light of those truths.

Two Kinds of People

Verse 11 of chapter 2 brings us to a point of transition in Paul's letter, and it would be wise now to review where we are. Chapter 2 presents Ephesians' theme of peace through grace in Jesus Christ. Verses 1–10 present the peace we have with

God as he reconciles us to himself. We were objects of wrath but now are objects of his mercy. We were in bondage to the world, the devil, and the flesh, but now we are God's workmanship. The rest of the chapter, starting in verse 11, speaks of peace on earth as God reconciles believers one to another in Christ. At the end of chapter 1, Paul prayed that we might know the riches of our salvation; in chapter 2 he spells these out as peace with God and peace with one another, all by God's grace in Jesus Christ.

Paul begins this new section by recognizing the division among us. It is said that there are two kinds of people: those who think there are two kinds of people and those who don't. Paul is the kind of person who thinks there are two kinds of people! He wants us to remember what we were before and what we now are in Christ. He writes, "Therefore remember that at one time you [were] Gentiles in the flesh, called 'the uncircumcision' by what is called the circumcision, which is made in the flesh by hands."

Whenever there is division, there is always name-calling. Children learn this unpleasant truth at school. Adults know it from politics, our family squabbles, and sometimes even church situations. The ancient world knew about this phenomenon as well, and Paul points to the chasm that most divided the ancient world—that between Jews and Gentiles. This division between them was highlighted by circumcision, the practice of removing the flesh of the male foreskin. Writing to the Ephesian Christians, people living in Asia Minor, Paul notes that by and large they were Gentiles, whom the Jews ridiculed as "the uncircumcision."

God had given circumcision to mark the Israelites as separate from the world and holy to God. The Israelites were to use their holiness to attract the pagan nations to the true God. Instead, the Jews used it as a mark of superiority and contempt for others. Far from caring for the spiritual state of the

Gentiles, the Jews rejoiced in their belief that Gentiles were created only to stoke the fires of hell. They would not converse with Gentiles. They even passed a law forbidding a Jew to help a Gentile woman in childbirth, since that would bring another Gentile into the world.[1]

Sadly, some Christians look down on irreligious people in a similar way. They consider them more to be shunned than to be won by the grace of Christ. That spirit is as offensive now as was the Jews' attitude toward the Gentiles. By referring to Gentiles as "the uncircumcision," the Jews were rejoicing in non-Jews' ignorance of God.

For their part, the Gentiles weren't wild about the Jews, either. They threw the insult back, calling them "the circumcision." Proud in their possession of Greek culture, the Gentiles looked down on everyone who did not participate in their way of life.

What mattered was not circumcision but the division, hatred, and warfare among men. Human beings will divide and fight over practically anything; for all our supposed progress in the centuries since Paul lived, the world has found no solution for this problem.

Without Christ

Notice what Paul says about circumcision, namely, that it was only something "made in the flesh by hands." Galatians 6:15 gave his clearest opinion: "Neither circumcision counts for anything, nor uncircumcision, but a new creation." The same is true with all religious traditions and rituals today: they have no value apart from their spiritual reality. In the case of the Jews, the physical circumcision was always meant to symbolize an inward devotion, not to serve as an outward source of pride. "Circumcise therefore the foreskin of your heart," Moses commanded them (Deut. 10:16).

If the Jews lacked an inward correspondence to circumcision, the Gentiles' uncircumcision accurately depicted their spiritual state. Thus Paul wants the Christians to realize how impoverished was their former position. Verse 12 reminds them: "Remember that you were at that time separated from Christ, alienated from the commonwealth of Israel and strangers to the covenants of promise." That is more than ancient history; it also depicts people today who live apart from God.

First, Paul says, "Remember that you were at that time separated from Christ." His point is not merely that before becoming Christians, they were without Jesus Christ; that much is obvious. But when speaking of Christ, he means "Messiah." They lacked any savior.

This was true of the Greek religion and worldview, as it is true of secular humanism today. If you read the ancient Greeks, you find that they had no hope for a savior. The Ephesians, for instance, lived in a city where the hideous goddess of fertility, Diana, or Artemis, was worshiped. If you purchased her favor, she supposedly might lend you the help of her power, but she offered no salvation from the great problems of life. Likewise, Greek philosophers had no idea of salvation. They viewed history as an endless cycle, with no purpose, no plan, and no destiny. In contrast, the Jews had a positive outlook on the future, despite their troubles. "Even in their bitterest days the Jews never doubted that the Messiah would come," one writer observes.[2]

Sadly, the Gentile worldview has become dominant in our society; we need to realize that today's new thinking is anything but new. A worldview answers questions that shape reality for us: What and where am I? What is the problem? What is the solution? Today's secular worldview, imported directly from the pagan ancient world, says that we are products of chance living without purpose on a random orb in space. The problem is how to just get by with as much pleasure and as little pain as possible. The answer is to look out for yourself. What could be more bleak and ignoble than that? But our society ignores the fact that this rampant individualism and selfishness is not working. This is why our cities are littered with the human refuse of an increasingly bankrupt society. This is why our most affluent suburbs are often scenes of the darkest despair and emptiness.

The Christian has a totally different worldview. He says, "I am made in the image of God, placed in the world of his making for his glory. The problem is sin, with its fruits of misery and death. But we have a real solution. We have a Savior, Jesus Christ, who has conquered sin and death on the cross. His resurrection is our victory, and we live in the power of his triumph." Unbelievers have no Christ, no salvation, no victory. The best they can do is to try to avoid reality. Christians have victory in Christ Jesus, our Savior.

Paul next points out that the Gentiles were "alienated from the commonwealth of Israel." Before Christ came and the gospel spread throughout the world, the little nation of Israel was alone the people of God. However great the Greeks and Romans might be, however much power or wealth, learning or glory they might acquire, they were still outside the circle of God's special love and care. Their days were numbered. To be saved, you had to be an Israelite in accordance with God's plan at that time in salvation history.

This point is illustrated by the relationship between Ruth and Naomi, told in the Old Testament. Ruth was a foreigner who married into Naomi's Jewish family. After a famine killed all the men, Naomi decided to go back to Israel to live in God's care. Ruth had apparently learned much about Israel's God during her time of marriage. When Naomi prepared to depart, Ruth appealed to her: "Do not urge me to leave you or to return from following you. For where you go I will go, and where you lodge I will lodge. Your people shall be my people, and your God my God" (Ruth 1:16). Notice how Ruth worded this statement. In order to say, "Your God [shall be] my God," she first had to say, "Your people shall be my people." She knew that she could not enter into God's salvation without entering into God's people.

Much has changed in light of the gospel, mainly that you do not have to be part of one nation or ethnic group. But you still cannot be saved without God's people becoming your people. Countless converts to Christ have learned that you cannot maintain all your old associations when you come to Christ and that you must enter into new ones. Above all, if you find the church a dull, unappealing society for which you have little interest or affection, you should reconsider the reality of your salvation.

We are living in a time when the church is held in low esteem, even among Christians. This is, I think, in part an overreaction to the religious formalism of a prior generation, and due also to the worldliness of so many professing believers. Our society is individualistic and consumeristic, so people think of the church in those terms as well. Christians have no fear of belittling or dividing the church, even though it is the commonwealth of God's own people. Our low view of God's household is evidenced by our church-shopping, church-hopping, and, for many, church-dropping.

But one of the greatest tragedies of being without Christ is being outside of his church. Martyn Lloyd-Jones writes, "By being 'without Christ' . . . you are outside that circle in which God is peculiarly interested. You do not belong to the covenant people. . . . Today it is the Christian Church that corresponds to the commonwealth of Israel. The most terrible thing about a man who is not a Christian is that he is outside that circle and does not belong to the people of God."[3]

Third, Paul calls the Gentiles "strangers to the covenants of promise." At different times in history, God made covenants with his people through such individuals as Abraham, Moses, and David. But interestingly, Paul mentions "promise" in the singular. There were many covenants, but one promise, one salvation, that God had always proclaimed. Geoffrey Wilson explains that the Gentiles "were ignorant of the *one* promise of salvation which God had confirmed to Abraham and his seed in several covenants."[4] That promise looked forward to and was fulfilled by the coming of Jesus Christ.

It is God's Word that records his covenants, but the Gentiles did not know or understand God's Word, just like people today who never come to church. That is why they were ignorant of God's promise. Lloyd-Jones points out that unbelievers today "can read their Bible and it does not move them. . . . They are strangers, they are like people from another country, they do not understand the language."[5] Does that describe you? Are you a stranger to the promises of the Bible, so that it all means nothing and makes no sense? Then you need to cry out to God that by his Holy Spirit he would give you eyes to see and a heart to understand.

Without Hope and Without God

This, Paul says, is the kind of people the Gentiles were, as are their modern-day unbelieving counterparts. Christians are to remember that this is the kind of people we were before God's grace came to us. He wants Christians to realize what a blessing it is to be part of God's church and recipients of God's covenant promise of salvation in Christ.

Paul completes verse 12 by detailing the kind of life that people lead apart from Christ. People may not mind being Gentiles or strangers to God, but the kind of life this alienation produces is not so good. Paul memorably describes them as "having no hope and without God in the world."

Possessing no idea of a savior, the Greeks suffered an epidemic hopelessness. The same is true of today's secular culture, which is increasingly overwhelmed by despair. This lack of hope relates to our attitude to both life and death.

People today lack hope in life, which is why so many lead a mindless pursuit of pleasure and entertainment. Neil Postman aptly chronicled this phenomenon in his book titled *Amusing Ourselves to Death.*[6] What is most depressing is that the few people who do think deeply are the most pessimistic people of all. Not all of them are highly educated. *Life* magazine ran an issue on the meaning of life. Jose Martinez, a taxi driver, offered this: "We're here to die, just live and die. . . . Life is a big fake. Nobody gives a damn. You're rich or you're poor. You're here, you're gone. You're like the wind. After you're gone, other people will come. . . . We're gonna destroy ourselves, nothing we can do about it."[7] For all our arrogant claims to achieving heaven on earth through materialistic progress, the reality is that, as Ravi Zacharias writes, "never before in history has such hopelessness enshrouded so many people, as the heart's deepest longings remain unmet."[8]

If secular people have no hope about life, things only get worse when it comes to death. The Gentiles of Paul's day had no hope for life after death, expecting only to lie in the ground, as one of their philosophers wrote, "bereft of life, voiceless as a stone."[9] The same is true of people in every age. It is those who flout God most in life who most despair in the face of death. Napoleon cried out on his deathbed, "I die before my time, and my body will be given back to the earth. . . . What an abyss between my deep misery and the eternal kingdom of Christ." The famous unbelieving philosopher Thomas Hobbes died saying, "If I had the whole world, I would give it to live one day. . . . I am about to take a leap into the dark." Then there is the French writer Voltaire. Teachers today love to have young students read his arrogant dismissal of Christianity. But they don't tell them about Voltaire's desperation in death. He cried out, "I am abandoned by God and man! I will give you half of what I am worth if you will give me six months' life."[10]

Compare that despair to the peace and joy that Christians experience in death. One of the countless examples is that of Rowland Taylor, one of the English Reformers who could easily have avoided being burned at the stake if he had only been willing to deny his faith in Jesus. A few days before his martyrdom, Taylor wrote to his family.

> I believe that they are blessed which die in the Lord. God careth for sparrows, and for the hairs of our heads. I have ever found Him more faithful and favourable than is any father or husband. Trust ye, therefore, in Him by the means of our dear Saviour Christ's merits. Believe, love, fear, and obey Him: pray to Him, for He hath promised to help. Count me not dead, for I shall certainly live and never die.

That is hope! Taylor concluded the letter by quoting Psalm 27: "The Lord is my Light and my Salvation, whom then shall I fear?"[11]

Paul concludes by telling us the reason that people live and die without hope, describing the Gentiles as "without God in the world." It was not strictly true that the Greeks had no religion and no gods. But you can be very religious and not have God. The Greeks had legions of gods, but none of them were true. None of them could save. None conveyed hope.

So it is today for all who trust the false god of success. Best-selling novelist Jack Higgins confessed, "When you get to the top, there's nothing there."[12] The same is true of those who trust the false god of money, which cannot buy joy, peace, or satisfaction; or the false god of beauty, which exacts a tyrannical service; or the false god of romance, which so often fades or betrays; or the false god of fame, fleeting and unfaithful. Only the true God, revealed in his Word, who saves us through Jesus Christ, can give the hope for which we long. Only of him can it be said, "You are my fortress, my strong salvation."

With Christ we have hope because we have the true and saving God, who entered the world to conquer sin and death. But as Charles Spurgeon sums it up, "Without Christ, though you be rich as Croesus, and famous as Alexander, and wise as Socrates, yet you are naked, and poor, and miserable, for you lack him by whom are all things, and for whom are all things, and who is himself all in all."[13]

Never Forget

Paul reminds us of these things because he wants believers to remember. "Never forget!" he seems to urge, what you were and what you have now in Christ. Because of God's grace, you have a Savior, you are a blessed member of the people of God, with the Bible's promises signed and sealed for you. This appeal to remember yields at least three applications.

First, the reason for us to remember these things is to stir up our gratitude to God. Cicero rightly said that "gratitude is the mother of every other virtue." If you are thankful to God, your heart will want to live for him. Remember what you were before God came to you in grace. Realize what you would be now and what would be your future destiny, were it not for God's gift in Jesus Christ. This is why Christians so greatly need the Bible's teaching on sin and judgment—not to put us down, but because if we do not realize what we were and what we deserved, we will never praise God as we should.

Second, unlike the Jews in their contempt for the hopeless, godless Gentiles, we are to look with mercy on those without hope and without God. We are no better; we are objects of God's mercy. Therefore, let us devote ourselves to that greatest of all mercies: a living, speaking witness about the salvation that God offers to everyone through faith in Jesus Christ.

Finally, never give in to despair if you are a Christian. Never let resentment take hold of you when you suffer or have unfulfilled desires. Never let temptation be your master. Never forget the grace of God. Remember what God has done for you already and at what cost to himself. Never doubt his saving love. And therefore live with courage and resolve, with hope and joy, knowing that you are part of a grand design to glorify God and enjoy him forever. Remember who you are and whose you are. Remember, and do not forget.

Questions for Study and Reflection

1. Why is *remembering* such an important part of a Christian's experience?
2. The author states that the apostle Paul presents two kinds of people. What are they? How is there division between the two kinds of people?
3. If you were converted as an adult, how do you now look back on your life when it was without Christ? What is it that Christians can know about others who are without Christ? How was Greek culture "Christ-less" and how is today's secular culture "Christ-less"?
4. What words does Paul use to describe the Christ-less life? How have you witnessed or experienced these things? What sorts of ministry opportunities does this situation suggest to believers?
5. What was God's solution for the hopelessness of our fallen world? What does God's solution say about God himself?

10

Brought Near to God

Ephesians 2:13

But now in Christ Jesus you who once were far off have been brought near by the blood of Christ.
—Ephesians 2:13

As we study the Bible, we occasionally want to ask not only *what* the Scripture is saying but also *why* it says what it says. This is especially true when it comes to a writer such as the apostle Paul, the premier missionary and theologian of the apostolic church, and to a book such as Ephesians, described by many as the crown of his writings. Surely the pastoral logic displayed here is significant for all believers.

The pastoral wisdom revealed by the apostle is different from the wisdom common in our day. If we ask people today,

"What do believers need to hear in order to grow spiritually and avoid the dangers of life?" most answers would be very different from those given by Paul. Most today would focus on techniques or behaviors that believers should engage in. Paul, in contrast, thinks we most need to know about God and what he has done for us in Christ. Paul's primary concern is always with theology: he believes that good theology produces godly thinking, which in turn leads to fruitful lives.

The tragedy today is that so few Christians are interested in theology, which is another way of saying that they are not interested in God. What people want to hear about is themselves, if not the personal life of the man in the pulpit. But notice how little attention the apostle pays to these things. Paul was God-centered in his thinking and his living, and he wants his readers to be God-centered as well.

A Great Contrast

This is what Paul is concerned with in making his first exhortation of Ephesians. "Remember!" he exhorts us. "Remember what God has done for you. Remember what you were apart from Christ and what you now are and have in Christ." Ephesians 2:11–12 gives the negative side of this equation, what we were apart from Christ: aliens to God's people, strangers to the covenants of promise, without hope and without God in the world. In verse 13 Paul turns to the positive: "But now in Christ Jesus you who once were far off have been brought near by the blood of Christ." Realize, he says, what you were saved from, what you are saved to, and what it is that saves you.

Why does Paul want us to focus on these things? Because doing this, explains Martyn Lloyd-Jones, is

> the only way whereby we can ever understand the greatness of this salvation; and as we do so it will lead to joy

> and rejoicing, to praise and thanksgiving to an assurance and a confidence in Christ which nothing can shake. But in order to come to that we have to realize two things. We have got to see what we were without Christ. Then we have to realize what is now true of us in the Lord Jesus Christ.[1]

Paul makes use of the illustration provided by the Israelite temple. The temple consisted of a series of areas of increasingly restricted access. In the center was the inner sanctum, the Most Holy Place. Only the high priest could enter this room, on only one day of the year. Outside the veil that separated this room was the Holy Place, where the priests served daily by keeping the candles lighted, the incense burning, and the table of showbread fresh. Outside the temple was the priests' court, where the altar for the burnt sacrifices was kept fired. Here also, only the priests could enter.

Around this area was a succession of porches. First was the Court of the Israelites, separated from the priestly area by only a low stone barrier. Ritually clean Israelite men could congregate here. Next, to the east, was the Women's Court, where Israelite women were free to come. Beyond this was the outer layer, the Court of the Gentiles, separated by a higher wall on which a warning was posted in both Greek and Latin, forbidding any Gentile to pass, on pain of death. This is probably what Paul refers to in verse 14 when he speaks about the dividing wall between the Jews and the Gentiles.

This tells us a couple of things. First, the Gentiles' real problem was not their separation from the Israelites, but their separation from God. That is what the wall of division showed. People outside of Christianity today have the same problem. Like the Gentiles of Paul's day, they are alienated from the true and living God. They do not know him or his promises, and they are not part of his people. This is why they have no solid basis for hope and no power to contend with sin and death. The best the Greeks could attain, like secular people today, was either a stoicism that embraced hopelessness or a hedonism that tried simply to avoid it. Paul's point to the Gentile Christians is that before they came to Christ, they were godless in the true sense of the word—and so it is for unbelievers today. The answers to life's questions are found only in God; the solution to life's problems comes only from God; the purpose that gives value to life is the blessing and glory of God. To these things they are ignorant and blind, and so were we before coming to God in Christ.

This illustration of the temple and its courts also tells us that there is an absolute difference between believers and nonbelievers. The Jews and Gentiles were alike in many ways, but there was this crucial, defining difference: the Gentiles were separated from God, whereas the Jews were brought near. Some Jews may have been closer to God than others, but they all had access to God as his people. Some Gentiles may have been further from God than others, but none of them could come into his presence. Here, then, is the difference that defines what Christianity is, and it is an absolute, objective difference. Jesus Christ brings people past the barrier—indeed, in terms of the temple illustration we are brought through every barrier, even within the veil of the Most Holy Place—to dwell in the light of God's presence and favor. All other people are outside, beyond the wall that is God's law, far from God, aliens from God's commonwealth, and strangers to the covenants of promise.

The key difference is not that Christians are better people or have improved themselves. This is an eventual by-product of Christianity, but not its defining reality. Many Christians are not better people, although God is working in them for righteousness. The difference is that union with Jesus Christ through faith changes the status of those who were "far off" from God and makes them those "brought near."

We might say that the whole purpose of the book of Ephesians is to make this point. Paul tells us in 2:12 what people apart from Christ lack, but elsewhere in the book he speaks of the corresponding blessings for all those in Christ. First, Paul points out that the Gentiles were "separated from Christ." But what of us? He says in Ephesians 1:13 that having "heard the word of truth, the gospel of your salvation, and believed in him," we now are "in Christ." In addition, the Gentiles were "alienated from the commonwealth of Israel" (2:12). But 2:19 proclaims that we now "are no longer strangers and aliens, but . . . are fellow citizens with the saints." We were "strangers to the covenants of promise," Paul reminds us. But in Ephesians 3:6 he writes that now, "the Gentiles are fellow heirs, members of the same body, and partakers of the promise in Christ Jesus through the gospel."

The contrast continues, with those apart from Christ described as "having no hope." Paul observes that the Jews "were the first to hope in Christ" but that now the Gentiles, having also believed, "were sealed with the promised Holy Spirit, who is the guarantee of our inheritance" (Eph. 1:12–14). Likewise, the Gentiles were "without God." But, Paul adds in 2:19, we are now "members of the household of God."

This is what Christianity is about! There are ultimately two kinds of people—and in the contrast, we see just how great is the blessing that God is offering to all the world through Jesus Christ, and how great is the salvation that we who believe have received by God's grace. Remember this, Paul exhorts, and it will change the way you live.

Brought Near

This contrast is designed to make us grateful to God, but also to instill in us the confidence we need. In two key words, "brought near," Paul cites the great privilege we now possess in Christ.

Implicit in these words is the idea that salvation is at its foremost reconciliation to God. We were alienated from God, but now we enter his household, becoming his children. A father is not responsible for every child in the world, but only for his own. He works to provide for all their needs, to provide them with a home, to put food on the table, to clothe and educate them. If you are a Christian, this is how things stand between you and God. You have been brought into his household, and God accepts a responsibility to care for your soul. This does not mean that nothing bad will ever happen to you, but rather that you will find God a ready provider in every situation. He will certainly discipline you as needed, for he is also responsible for that. But he will not neglect those things you need, and he will secure your future, growth, and protection. People glibly talk about God's being the Father of everyone, but the Bible flatly denies such a concept. According to John 1:12, "all who did receive [Jesus], who believed in his name, he gave the right to become children of God."

Paul's main idea here is access to God. Children have access to their father, and Christians have open access to heaven's throne. Even the Old Testament priests were separated from direct contact with God's presence by the veil that separated the Most Holy Place. But the simplest Christian has greater access than they ever did because the veil is removed in Jesus Christ. In Christ we have permanent and open access to God in prayer, certain of his gracious reception because we who were far off have been brought near through the superior priesthood of Christ.

Best of all, having been brought near to God in Christ, we begin a relationship with God. We come to know God—who he is and what he is like. Not only do we learn things *about* him, but we grow in a personal relationship *with* him. This is the chief of God's covenant promises: "I will be their God, and they shall be my people. . . . They shall all know me" (Heb. 8:10–11, quoting Jer. 31:33–34). We now realize this truth only in part, but Revelation 21:3–4 displays the fullness of this blessing as it will unfold in eternity: "He will dwell with them, and they will be his people, and God himself will be with them as their God. He will wipe away every tear from their eyes, and death shall be no more, neither shall there be mourning, nor crying, nor pain anymore, for the former things have passed away."

By His Blood

Most importantly, Paul tells us what has produced this great change, enabling us, those who were far from God, to be brought near into such blessing: "Now in Christ Jesus you who once were far off have been brought near by the blood of Christ" (Eph. 2:13).

Reconciliation is needed when there has been a breach between two parties. The breach between us and God is our sin. God has a cause for offense with us; there is an issue that must be resolved before we can be restored to his fellowship and blessing. God is holy, and the offense of our sin stands between us and him. Even in human relationships, if there is a real and deep-seated problem between two people, they will not be able to get together—not really, not wholeheartedly, not permanently—until the matter is resolved. One writer therefore observes, "If God and man are to be reconciled, it cannot be by the simple expedient of ignoring sin, but only by overcoming it."[2]

How, then, did God resolve the problem of our sin and thus reconcile us to himself? Paul's answer: "by the blood of Christ." There has been an atonement. A sacrifice for sin has been offered that is acceptable to God; indeed, it was the sacrifice of God's own appointing, for which he sent his Son into the world. Paul writes in 2 Corinthians 5:19 that "in Christ God was reconciling the world to himself, not counting their trespasses against them." He explains, "[God] made him to be sin who knew no sin, so that in him we might become the righteousness of God." Therefore, he urges, "We implore you on behalf of Christ, be reconciled to God" (2 Cor. 5:20–21).

Matthew 27:51 relates that when Jesus died on the cross, the veil in the temple was torn from top to bottom. That veil was the most holy of all barriers, the one that kept even the priests from direct contact with God. Its rending declares that now all may come to God through faith in the blood of Christ, that is, in Christ's death for our sin.

This is good news for everyone, regardless of who and what you are. By his blood, Christ has opened wide the way to God. But notice that Christ's blood is the one and only way by which you may come to God. Paul does not tell us that we may come to God simply by virtue of being made in his image, for mankind is marred and shamed by sin. He does not say that you may come to God by being a good person. This is what people mainly think today, and it is a fatal error. In God's eyes you are not a good person, and ironically, only our self-serving, sin-stained perspective allows us to think that we are good. "No one does good," God says, "not even one" (Rom. 3:12, quoting Ps. 14:3). Paul does not teach that you may draw near to God through religion, by being a devout person, by partaking in rituals, or by the sacraments alone. No mystical experience, however spiritual it may make you feel, will overcome the barrier of your sin. Only the blood of Christ can reconcile you to God and bring you near to him. Jesus reconciles us to God and brings us near not by good intentions, not simply by telling us that God is love, and not by preaching the Sermon on the Mount, but by dying in our place as an atonement for our sin.

In one of his greatest parables, Jesus makes this point vividly clear. Two men came to the temple to pray. One was a Pharisee, the religious elite of Judaism, and the other was a tax collector, the spiritual scum of the nation. Jesus tells us that the Pharisee stood before God, saying, "God, I thank you that I am not like other men, extortioners, unjust, adulterers, or even like this tax collector." Having boasted about who he was, he proceeded to boast about what he did: "I fast twice a week; I give tithes of all that I get." He was confident that because of his pedigree, his morality, and his religion, God was certain to receive him. The tax collector's approach to God was altogether different: "But the tax collector, standing far off, would not even lift up his eyes to heaven, but beat his breast, saying, 'God, be merciful to me, a sinner!'" (Luke 18:10–13). The expression "be merciful to me" has explicit reference to the sacrifices offered in the temple; literally, it is "be mercy-seated to me," the mercy seat being the place where the atoning blood was offered to God.

In whose shoes would you rather be? Who do you think was more likely to be received by God? Was it the moral and religious man, the man from the good family and the right connections, who came forward on the basis of these traits? Or was it the man who admitted that he was a failure, who could only beat his breast and ask God to forgive his sins through atoning blood? Jesus concluded: "I tell you, this man"—the tax collector—"went down to his house justified, rather than the other" (Luke 18:14). The reason is that, being sinners, we are brought near only "by the blood of Christ."

This is the great reality that applies to everyone, as Paul explains in Romans 3:22–25: "There is no distinction: for all have sinned and fall short of the glory of God, and are justified by his grace as a gift, through the redemption that is in Christ Jesus, whom God put forward as a propitiation by his blood, to be received by faith."

Jesus died as a propitiation, that is, by his own blood turning away God's wrath from those who trust in him. People believe in many things, but only one thing saves us; only one thing brings us near to God and restores us to his love. That is faith in Christ's blood: his atoning death for our forgiveness and reconciliation to God. If you believe that, if you trust only in the death of God's Son to bring you to the Father, then you who were far away, without hope and without God, are now one of God's beloved children. You may not be the person you should be, and you may be weighed down with a sense of your unworthiness. But in Christ, God's blessing and love are yours and will remain yours not because you earned them but because Christ earned them for you. They were purchased, as the apostle Peter explains, "not with perishable things such as silver or gold, but with the precious blood of Christ" (1 Peter 1:18–19). Therefore, you may stop trying to win your place in God's favor and stop fretting about your salvation, instead resting secure, knowing that though you were far away, and deservedly so, Christ's blood has reconciled you to God.

Through Gates of Splendor

Paul's teaching in this verse begs a question, and nothing else matters compared to it. Are you separated from Christ in unbelief, or are you in Christ and with Christ through faith in his blood? It is literally a life-or-death matter, with everlasting consequences. Being with or without Christ is what makes all the difference eternally.

I often think of the scene at Jesus' death, his cross standing between the crosses of two other men. The two men crucified with Jesus represent all of humanity, and like all of us they had one thing in common. They were both guilty men ripe for a just condemnation. "There is no distinction," Paul says, "for all have sinned" (Rom. 3:22–23). But there was one difference between them, a difference that divides humanity into its two basic groups: one of the criminals cried out to Jesus for salvation. He was not a good person, and he was unable to do any good works or earn salvation in any way. He was already affixed to a cross. But by faith alone he cried out to Jesus. Jesus told him, "Truly, I say to you, today you will be with me in Paradise" (Luke 23:43). Likewise, today, every sinner who calls in faith to the sin-bearing Savior gains immediate forgiveness and is reconciled to God. The other thief rejected Jesus, mocked him, and perished in his sins, to receive on his own soul the eternal punishment that he and all those like him deserve. Those are the two kinds of people in this world. Which kind are you?

This is the contrast that Paul speaks of. If you are a Christian, it does not mean that all your troubles are gone and everything will be rosy from now on. But it does mean that you are no longer far from God: condemned, estranged, and barred from his blessings. You have been brought near in Christ. Now, in your weakness, though you are prone to failure and sin, you may rely on Christ's blood to be certain of God's favor. And through Christ's blood you have access to God's grace so that you will grow stronger as you walk in faith, and you will gain power against sin as you turn to God in prayer, as your mind is transformed by God's Word, and as you worship together with God's people.

Paul reminds these Gentile Christians of the wall that once separated them from God. The Bible ends with a picture of the heavenly city to come, and it, too, is surrounded by a wall. The apostle John writes in Revelation: "I saw no temple in the city, for its temple is the Lord God the Almighty and the Lamb. And the city has no need of sun or moon to shine on it, for the glory of God gives it light, and its lamp is the Lamb" (Rev. 21:22–23).

This is the destination of all those now brought near to God in Christ. Of these things we may now partake spiritually through God's Word, prayer, and our worship of God together.

But as I said, it is a city with a wall. So how do you get in? How will you come to God in the everlasting age to come? The Bible's last chapter tells us: "Blessed are those who wash their robes, so that they may have the right to the tree of life and that they may enter the city by the gates" (Rev. 22:14). Only those, but all of those, who are washed clean in the blood of Christ may enter, drawing near to God and his blessings forever.

I mentioned that the walls around Israel's temple were marked with warnings for the Gentiles to stay out, on pain of death. But the walls of this city, the city in which shines the light of Jesus Christ forever, are marked not with a warning but with an invitation for all to come by faith in his gospel. Jesus himself, who died to bring us near by his blood, gives the invitation to all. "Come," he says. "Whoever is thirsty, let him come; and whoever wishes, let him take the free gift of the water of life" (Rev. 22:17 NIV).

Jesus invites you now to come near to God through faith in his blood, though you have been far away in sin and unbelief. If you will come, you will be reconciled to God, forgiven of your sins, and received with love as God's precious child, to live forever with him.

Questions for Study and Reflection

1. What are Christians saved from? Saved to? Who saves us and how?
2. How does the Jewish temple help us to understand what it means to be "brought near" to God?
3. What is the key difference between a Christian and a non-Christian? What difference does it make that we are "brought near" to God by Christ?
4. The author states that the expression "brought near" leads us to realize our great privileges in Christ. What are these privileges? How do we understand our membership in God's household and what are its blessings?
5. Paul says that believers are brought near to God "by the blood of Christ." How does Christ's blood reconcile sinners to God? Why is this the way that God saves sinners? Why do some people respond negatively to the atoning blood of Christ? How would you respond to criticisms of God's way of salvation, through his Son's precious blood?

11

Christ, Our Peace

Ephesians 2:14

For he himself is our peace.
—Ephesians 2:14

If there is one thing our world needs, it is peace. In political elections, we often hear of platforms dedicated to "peace and prosperity." Prosperity flows from peace, so a leader who can bring about peace, however temporary, is bound to be popular and successful.

One strategy for making peace is the use of the sword. This was the way of the ancient Roman empire. Augustus Caesar, returning from his conquest of western Europe, dedicated a great temple of peace in his own name, placing it on the Campus Martius in Rome, the Field of Mars, the Roman god of war. The point was that war is the way to peace. It was, however, peace for some and the sword for others. The ancient historian Tacitus commented of Rome: "To plunder, butcher, steal, these things they misname Empire; they make a desolation and call it peace."[1] Those who live by the sword die by the sword. The day finally came when the sword fell on Rome, and the statue that Augustus had erected to himself as peacemaker was torn down; all that remains of it now is a broken-off little finger.

Another approach to peace is diplomacy. This may be a more virtuous strategy than war, but it is hardly more successful. Its failure is vividly displayed by the ceaseless round of Mideast peace treaties today, none of which makes the slightest dent in the never-ending violence. Without changing the hatred, what they call peace is really a truce in which both sides reload for the next round of war. Most symbolic of the diplomatic approach is the statement of British Prime Minister Neville Chamberlain after his meeting with Adolf Hitler in 1938. While German factories were pouring out tanks and bombers, Chamberlain boasted, "We have achieved peace in our time." Soon those tanks and bombers were unleashed, and his era of "peace" was bathed in sorrow and blood.

Neither war nor diplomacy can ever achieve a true and lasting peace, which is why mankind has made absolutely no progress in this matter. Jeremiah complained of the false prophets, "'Peace, peace,' they say, when there is no peace" (Jer. 6:14 NIV). So it is today. But whereas mankind has failed, Jesus Christ proclaimed on the eve of his death a victory over sin that produces true and lasting peace. "Peace I leave with you," Jesus claimed. "My peace I give to you. Not as the world gives do I give to you" (John 14:27).

The most profound teaching in the Bible on how Jesus Christ gives peace is found in Ephesians 2:14–18, which begins with the great statement: "For he himself is our peace."

Sin Results in Conflict

According to the Bible, conflict is the result of sin. We lack and so greatly need peace because of sin and its effects.

One reason for this is that God made the world in righteousness, and sin, by definition, is a violation of God's law and therefore of the way that God ordered the world for blessing. This reminds us that God's law—the Ten Commandments, for instance—is not just an arbitrary set of rules made to keep us from having fun. Rather, God was setting down what is wrong and harmful in the world he made. The second tablet of the Ten Commandments, numbers five through ten, deals with things that cause conflict and harm. "Honor your father and your mother. . . . You shall not murder. You shall not commit adultery. You shall not steal. You shall not [lie]. You shall not covet" (Ex. 20:12–17). When those commandments are broken—when we sin—the result is conflict and pain.

Another reason why sin causes conflict is that at the heart of sin is selfishness. Sin compels you to gain for yourself at the expense of others. The apostle James explains: "What causes quarrels and what causes fights among you? Is it not this, that your passions are at war within you? You desire and do not have, so you murder. You covet and cannot obtain, so you fight and quarrel" (James 4:1–2).

Another reason why sin causes conflict is that God curses sin. The first sin took place in Genesis 3, when Adam and Eve disobeyed God and ate of the tree of the knowledge of good and evil. God responded with curses that promised conflict. He promised enmity between the seed of the serpent and the seed of the woman, that is, between the unbelieving world and God's people (Gen. 3:15). He promised conflict between the man and woman in their marital union (Gen. 3:16) and even conflict between mankind and the created world: "Cursed is the ground because of you," he told Adam. "In pain you shall eat of it all the days of your life" (Gen. 3:17).

Conflict and misery because of sin is the story of the generations that followed. Genesis 4 tells us that because of jealousy and resentment, the first son ever born into the human race, Cain, murdered his younger brother, Abel. Cain's descendants were makers of war; the first human song ever recorded (Gen. 4:23–24) was written by Lamech to celebrate his killing of a man who had started a fight with him. Genesis 11 takes us forward into history, when all mankind united in a sinful desire to build the Tower of Babel in rebellion against God. God rewarded their sin with even more division, confusing their languages and scattering them abroad as a punishment.

Sin destroys peace on three basic levels. The first and most important is between man and God. This truth is vividly depicted in Genesis 3, when Adam and Eve respond to the first sin by fleeing from God. Paul begins his most detailed teaching of the gospel, in the book of Romans, with this stark reality: "The wrath of God is revealed from heaven against all ungodliness and unrighteousness of men" (Rom. 1:18).

Sin also destroys peace within ourselves. Isaiah 57:21 relates, "'There is no peace,' says my God, 'for the wicked.'" The prophet elaborates in vivid language: "The wicked are like the tossing sea; for it cannot be quiet, and its waters toss up mire and dirt" (v. 20). The sea is never at rest because it is pulled by the magnetic force of two contrary powers, the earth and the moon. Sin does the same to us: it is a power that gets hold of us and pulls us. But however we may want him to, God never goes away. However much man may reject God or disbelieve in God, we are still made in his image, with the reality of his moral order to contend with. Therefore, the voice of conscience speaks against the pull of sin, and we are gripped by a restless inner turmoil.

Finally, sin destroys peace in our relationships with others. I have already shown how this worked out in the early chapters of Genesis. But the relationship between Adam and Eve sufficiently makes the point. Before they sinned, our first parents lived in harmony and love. "The man and his wife were both naked and were not ashamed" (Gen. 2:25). But as soon as they sinned, they not only felt shame and put on fig leaves, but immediately entered into conflict. When God confronted Adam for eating the forbidden fruit, Adam became the first of a long line of male blame-shifters. Using both hands that God had given him—one to point at Eve and the other to point at God—Adam replied, "The woman whom you gave to be with me, she gave me fruit of the tree, and I ate" (Gen. 3:12). Adam was thus alienated both from God and from his wife, Eve.

At the root of all our conflict is sin. James Montgomery Boice explains, "The enemy of peace is not a lack of negotiations but the fundamental alienation that exists between every individual and God. It is because we are at enmity with God—that is the true meaning of sin—that we are also inevitably at enmity with ourselves, one another, and in a certain sense, with all the world."[2]

Salvation Brings Peace

The Bible teaches that redemption remedies the fall; salvation repairs what is ruined by sin. This means that if sin brings conflict, then salvation restores peace.

When the Bible speaks of peace, it means not just the absence of conflict, but the presence of harmony and blessing. The idea is fully expressed by the Old Testament word *shalom.* *Shalom* is the peace that comes from God. It is what the Levitical priests spoke of in their benediction:

> The Lord bless you and keep you;
> The Lord make his face to shine upon you and be
> gracious to you;

> The LORD lift up his countenance upon you and give you peace. (Num. 6:24–26)

This peace *from* God is possible only when we have peace *with* God. The barrier between us and God is our sin. Salvation brings the cure to sin. Salvation gives us forgiveness so that we are justified in God's sight, and it overthrows the power of sin in our hearts so that our hostility to God is replaced with faith and love. As Paul says, "Since we have been justified by faith, we have peace with God through our Lord Jesus Christ" (Rom. 5:1).

The theological term for this idea is *reconciliation.* Paul teaches in 2 Corinthians 5:18–21 that God sent Christ into the world to reconcile lost sinners to himself: "In Christ God was reconciling the world to himself, not counting their trespasses against them. . . . For our sake he made him to be sin who knew no sin, so that in him we might become the righteousness of God." Philip Graham Ryken reminds us:

> Reconciliation teaches something remarkable about the character of God. He befriends his enemies. He loves those who hate him. He offers peace to those who have waged war against him. Although he is the one who has been wronged, he is the one who makes things right. He does all this while the battle still rages. "When we were God's enemies, we were reconciled to him through the death of his Son." (Rom. 5:10)[3]

A good example of how peace *with* God gives us peace *from* God is found in the life of the Old Testament patriarch Jacob. His name meant "Grasper," and his whole life was spent grasping for things that his sinful heart wanted. He sought generally good things, but he sought them in the wrong ways and with wrong motives. As a result, he got no blessing and no peace. Jacob gained his father's covenant blessing by lying and cheating his elder brother, Esau; he gained his riches by tricking his father-in-law to take possession of the strongest animals in his herds. Along with his new possessions, he gained resentment and conflict. God came to him one night when Jacob's enemies were closing in on him. God wrestled with Jacob, bringing his heart into submission. Finally Jacob, having spent his whole life trying to place his hands on the blessings he wanted, instead put them onto God. He cried out to God, "I will not let you go unless you bless me" (Gen. 32:26). That was what God wanted: for Jacob to put his faith in him. God changed his heart, and from that time forward Jacob knew a peace and blessing that he had never had before. God does the same for everyone who gains peace with him through faith in Christ.

Salvation gives us peace with God, peace in our hearts, and, finally, peace with other people. I mentioned that God came to Jacob at a time when Jacob was lonely and defeated. His father-in-law was chasing him from behind, and as Jacob returned to his homeland, his brother Esau was waiting for him with superior forces. Jacob tried to bribe Esau with the sheep and goats and cattle that he had acquired from his wife's father, but he knew that these could not overcome Esau's hatred. He was outnumbered militarily, and diplomacy was not going to work. But after Jacob had wrestled with God and come to peace with him, he was able to admit his faults and come to his brother, asking forgiveness. God put his own love into Esau's heart, and the brothers, long estranged, were united in peace (see Gen. 32–33).

Peace is possible only when sin is overcome and removed. Salvation means being justified with God through faith in Christ, and thereby we have peace with him. His righteousness works in our lives, so harmony and wholeness begin to replace conflict and brokenness. When we come together in righteousness and truth, we have peace with one another. The apostle John explained, "If we walk in the light, as he is in the light, we have fellowship with one another, and the blood of Jesus his Son cleanses us from all sin" (1 John 1:7).

He Is Our Peace

Paul brings all these ideas together with the powerful statement of our verse. Speaking of our Lord Jesus Christ, he says, "He himself is our peace" (Eph. 2:14). It is because of Christ's work for us and our relationship with him that we receive peace and have peace to give.

When Paul says of Christ that "he himself is our peace," he is remembering one of the great prophecies of Jesus' birth. Best known to us is that of Isaiah 9:6–7: "For to us a child is born, to us a son is given; and the government shall be upon his shoulder, and his name shall be called Wonderful Counselor, Mighty God, Everlasting Father, Prince of Peace. Of the increase of his government and of peace there will be no end. . . ." This is why on the night of Jesus' birth the angels sang, "Glory to God in the highest, and on earth peace among those with whom he is pleased!" (Luke 2:14).

Less well known is the prophecy that Paul quotes in Ephesians 2:14, from Micah chapter 5. That passage begins with a prophecy regarding the town of Bethlehem: "You, O Bethlehem Ephrathah, who are too little to be among the clans of Judah, from you shall come forth for me one who is to be ruler in Israel, whose coming forth is from of old, from ancient days" (Mic. 5:2). The prophet had foretold a day when the Jews would be conquered as God's judgment for their sin. But he promised that a ruler would rise up in a humble place, one who would be a divine Savior, "whose coming forth is from of old, from ancient days." Looking forward with amazing specificity to the coming of Jesus Christ, Micah prophesied that "he shall stand and shepherd his flock in the strength of the LORD, in the majesty of the name of the LORD his God. And they shall dwell secure, for now he shall be great to the ends of the earth. And he shall be their peace" (Mic. 5:4–5).

This is what it means to come to Christ in faith: to have him lead you through life as a faithful shepherd, one who died for the sheep, so that even in a world without peace we can live securely, knowing that our eternal destiny is assured and our present life held in the hands of a loving God. Jesus himself is our peace. John Calvin observes, "This is a beautiful title of Christ: the Peace between God and men. Let no one doubt that God is favourable to him if he remains in Christ."[4]

Paul has depicted man's relationship with God in terms of the Old Testament temple, with its series of barriers separating sinners from God's holy presence. Most important was the thick veil separating everyone—even the priests—from God's inner chamber. But where the veil once barred us from God, Jesus now stands, inviting us into God's blessing. He is the Mediator who brings peace, the veil's having split at the moment of his death (Matt. 27:51). He is also the Mediator in our hearts, standing between us and the turmoil caused by our sin. And he stands between us and other people, giving us grace to forgive, serve, and love—to make peace by the power of Jesus Christ. In all these ways, as Psalm 29:11 tells us, "The LORD blesses his people with peace" (NIV).

Living the Peace of Christ

So here is the question: do you have this peace? Are you experiencing and making peace? It is Christ who gives us peace and is our peace.

It is Christ who brings peace and love to marriages. Sin brought conflict between Adam and Eve, just as it does to couples today. The Bible tells wives to submit to their husbands, to respect them, and to minister for their blessing. But women say, "You don't know my husband. He isn't worthy of respect.

He doesn't do what he is supposed to do." Therefore, there is conflict, hostility, resentment. But Christ is our peace. Because of their relationship to Christ and by the power he sends, wives can build up their husbands with respect and encouragement because they want to honor Jesus and they trust God to bless what he has commanded. Husbands are told to love their wives as Christ loved the church, to sacrifice for their well-being, to cherish them and minister to the needs of their hearts. But men say, "You don't know my wife. We're not compatible. We don't get along." So let Christ be your peace. Remember his love for you, and give it to your wife in his name. Forgive as the Lord forgave you. Pray with and for your wife because Christ died for you and God brought you together in marriage. Let Jesus stand within your marriage, bringing you together in love and mutual ministry because Christ is your peace.

The same is true in the workplace, neighborhoods, and families. Our lives are filled with conflict and embittered by resentment and hostility. If someone sins against you, let Christ be your peace. Forgive the person and do good to him or her. Peter writes, "For to this you have been called, because Christ also suffered for you, leaving you an example, so that you might follow in his steps. He committed no sin, neither was deceit found in his mouth. When he was reviled, he did not revile in return; when he suffered, he did not threaten, but continued entrusting himself to him who judges justly" (1 Peter 2:21–23).

The same is true with circumstances. Bad news comes. Disaster strikes. Our hearts start filling with anxiety and turmoil. Let Christ be your peace. Remember that he who stilled the winds and the waves reigns now on high for you. Remember that your loving God is sovereign over all things. Turn to Christ, trust in him, and hear his voice in your heart, "Peace! Be still!" (Mark 4:39).

Christ is our peace, especially as we turn to him in prayer—when faced with conflict or anxiety, when tempted to sin, or when sinned against. Paul writes in Philippians 4:6–7, "Do not be anxious about anything, but in everything by prayer and supplication with thanksgiving let your requests be made known to God. And the peace of God, which surpasses all understanding, will guard your hearts and your minds in Christ Jesus."

But the most important question is this: Do you have peace with God? Without peace *with* God, you can never know the peace *of* God, the peace God gives. Even if you should cruise through life without major problems, if you are not right with God, eternity will hold no peace for you. We enter this world as members of a race at war with God. Whether we acknowledge it or not, in our sin we have taken up arms against the Most High. Until we have peace with God, we are living on the fault line of a great earthquake that shakes us even now and will soon break apart in the final judgment.

But Christ is our peace with God. He does what man can never do, what no sword can impose and no treaty can enforce. Christ has removed the cause of conflict and hostility, and he is undoing the effects of sin in the lives of those who trust him. Jesus fulfilled for us the law we have broken. He has removed the veil and every barrier that stands between us and the light of God. He sends the Spirit to work the love of God into our hearts. He is the sacrifice who atoned for our sins and the priest who takes us by the hands and brings us as children into God's family and worshipers into God's presence. Christ is our peace with God, and therefore within ourselves, and thereby with other people and with the changing circumstances of life.

The Song of Peace

I mentioned earlier that the prophecies of Jesus speak of him as Prince of Peace, and that the angels sang of peace on the night of his birth. I want to conclude with another instance, involving Zechariah, the father of John the Baptist, when he realized that the birth of his son meant that the Messiah was soon to follow. He prophesied by the Holy Spirit, singing of the peace for which the world had so desperately longed through all the war-torn, anguished centuries, which was finally coming to change the world. "Blessed be the Lord God of Israel," he sang, "for he has visited and redeemed his people." Because of "the tender mercy of our God," Jesus Christ was coming, "to give light to those who sit in darkness and in the shadow of death, to guide our feet into the way of peace" (Luke 1:68, 78–79).

That song can be yours if you will come in faith to Jesus Christ, and receive the gift of peace that God has offered us through him. If you will be his disciple, trusting him and making his Word the rule for your life, you will have found the path to peace. He will give you peace. He will be your peace. And he will use you to bring peace to a hurting, dying world.

Questions for Study and Reflection

1. What are the world's strategies for making peace, and how does Jesus' approach to peace-making differ? Explore Paul's statement "He himself is our peace."
2. How is sin at the root of conflict? How does this work, and what are some biblical examples of sin producing strife and conflict?
3. How does salvation in Christ lead to peace? Have you had experiences with Christian faith reconciling people who had been in strife?
4. The author states that Paul has the Jerusalem temple in mind when he says that Christ is "our peace." What is the point of this comparison? How does Jesus make peace between us and God?
5. Is it important that Christians experience peace in their personal lives? In their relationships with others? How can we pursue peace in Christ's name?

12

The New Humanity

Ephesians 2:14–16

For he himself is our peace, who has made us both one and has broken down in his flesh the dividing wall of hostility by abolishing the law of commandments expressed in ordinances, that he might create in himself one new man in place of the two, so making peace.
—Ephesians 2:14–15

Genesis chapter 11 records one of the great culminating moments in human history. Adam and Eve had fallen into sin, and the result was the violence depicted in the early chapters of Genesis. In chapter 11, mankind is united once more, joined in rebellion against God in an attempt to usurp his glory.

Genesis 11 begins, "Now the whole earth had one language and the same words. . . . They said, 'Come, let us build ourselves a city and a tower with its top in the heavens, and let us make a name for ourselves'" (Gen. 11:1, 4). This was, of course, all part of the devil's subtle plan and an imitation of his own failed attempt to overthrow God's rule. God, stooping down to this puny venture, confused their language, "and from there the LORD dispersed them over the face of all the earth" (Gen. 11:9). This was how the human race became scattered across the globe, divided into cultures and peoples and nations at war.

So it was with the human race from the Tower of Babel until the coming of Jesus Christ. Jesus came to undo the effects of sin, including the Tower of Babel. As John states, "The reason the Son of God appeared was to destroy the works of the devil" (1 John 3:8). Therefore, if Genesis 11 is the culmination of the effects of sin, we should expect to see its reversal with Jesus' coming into the world.

Indeed, we discover this very thing in the book of Acts. On the day of Pentecost, just weeks after the resurrection of Christ and days after his ascension into heaven, the Holy Spirit was poured out by Christ on his church. In that gathering were men from all the nations and languages created in judgment at Babel, now brought together by the Spirit of God. When the apostle Peter began preaching and the tongues of fire fell on them, "they were amazed and astonished, saying, . . . 'How is it that we hear, each of us in his own native language?' . . . And all were amazed and perplexed, saying to one another, 'What does this mean?'" (Acts 2:7–12).

What did it mean? It meant the coming of peace in Jesus Christ to the scattered tribes of men. This is something that Paul wants the readers of Ephesians to understand. They were Gentiles living in Asia Minor. They had been, as verse 12 says, "separated from Christ, alienated from the commonwealth of Israel and strangers to the covenants of promise, having no hope and without God in the world." Now, in Christ, they have been "brought near by the blood of Christ" (v. 13), reconciled to God by the cross. But there is something more for them to know and experience, namely, that the never-ending war brought on by sin has now been won. We are at peace with God, yes, but we can also have peace with men. Ephesians 2:16 states that Christ reconciled us to God in such a way that he brought us together "in one body through the cross, thereby killing the hostility." Here, Paul proclaims good news of peace: peace made possible through Christ's death, peace made real through Christ's resurrection, and peace experienced in the new humanity that is the body of Christ.

Peace Made Possible by Christ's Death

We know that Christ's death reconciles believers to God. This is what Paul emphasized in verse 13: "You who once were far off have been brought near by the blood of Christ." But as his teaching continues, he points out that Christ's death also makes peace possible within the human race.

The reason is given in verse 14. Paul speaks of the fundamental division within humanity, that between Jews and Gentiles. This was an outworking of the division created by God back in Genesis 3:15. God cursed the serpent, saying, "I will put enmity between you and the woman, and between your offspring and her offspring." This enmity was a provision of mercy and of protection for God's people. Without enmity with evil, they would become part of the sinful world and be absorbed in the rebellion against God. Their preservation, and thus that of the holy seed who would be their Savior, required that there be hostility between the people of God and the people of the world. In the time of the New Testament, this division was that between the Jews and the Gentiles as mandated by the Old Testament legal code.

Paul refers to "the dividing wall of hostility," created by "the law of commandments expressed in ordinances." In a previous chapter we recalled the physical wall that kept Gentiles out of the temple courts, with warnings that threatened death to any who might cross. This seems to be in Paul's mind as a symbol for the whole system of rules designed to keep Jews separate from Gentiles. They could not sit down to a meal with Gentiles or even eat the same foods. They dressed differently. They could not intermarry or enter into real friendships. To the Gentiles, this made the Jews seem strange and aloof. And the Jews came to regard the Gentiles as unclean and inferior.

Paul explains that Jesus abolished all this separation and broke down the wall "in his flesh." This refers to his atoning death on the cross. Before Jesus' coming, the system of the Old Testament law was the means by which the Jewish people entered into and expressed their relationship to God. No one else could come near to God. But as Paul explains in Galatians 3:23–29, all of that was a temporary measure to preserve the integrity of the covenant people until the Messiah should come. Jesus' coming abolished the administration of the Mosaic law and achieved access to God through his death. Here is how Paul explains it in Galatians: "The law was our guardian until Christ came, in order that we might be justified by faith. But now that faith has come, we are no longer under a guardian, for in Christ Jesus you are all sons of God, through faith. . . . There is neither Jew nor Greek, there is neither slave nor free, there is no male and female, for you are all one in Christ Jesus" (Gal. 3:24–28).

Christianity was able to quickly become a worldwide religion, as God intended, in part because cultural barriers could be overcome by the grace and truth of the gospel. Once the apostles understood that Christianity is to transcend every human division, they vigorously opposed every attempt to force Jewish cultural practices on Gentile converts. Anyone could become a child of God, just as they were, through a living faith in Jesus Christ.

Jesus himself foreshadowed this truth when he sat down on a well next to a Samaritan woman, recorded in John 4. She was amazed because no Jewish man would ever sit and talk with a Gentile woman, much less ask her to give him a drink, as Jesus did. Jesus spoke to her about the living water he provides to all who believe. In response to her puzzlement, Jesus said, "The hour is coming, and is now here, when the true worshipers will worship the Father in spirit and truth, for the Father is seeking such people to worship him" (John 4:23). That woman became the first evangelist to the Samaritans; people heard about Jesus and came to him, crying, "We know that this is indeed the Savior of the world" (4:42).

When Paul says that Jesus abolished the law, he does not mean the moral law, such as the Ten Commandments, which expresses God's unchangeable character. Jesus himself said, "Do not think that I have come to abolish the Law or the Prophets; I have not come to abolish them but to fulfill them" (Matt. 5:17). Likewise, God's people today are to obey God's moral law. But we are no longer to uphold those temporary regulations that separated Jews from Gentiles and protected God's people from contact with unbelievers.

This is a vital matter today, when too many Christians think holiness is about checking out of the culture. Many Christians think they are being holy if they have no non-Christian friends, if they enjoy only Christian entertainment, if they have nothing to do with their neighbors or treat their unbelieving coworkers as unclean. But Christ's death has freed God's people from the juvenile bonds of such legalism; we now are to go out into the world, being in the world but not of it, as the salt that preserves it from death and the light that shines in the darkness. Jesus treated the woman by the well as a person of dignity and worth; though she was a Samaritan, he asked her to do a service for him. Though he was the very kind of person she had learned to hate, she was drawn to him because of his combination of grace and truth.

Christ's death has made peace within this world possible, through the gospel of his salvation. We are now his ambassadors, not of judgment and wrath but of the reconciliation that God offers to all. As Paul said, so we say today, "We are ambassadors for Christ, God making his appeal through us. We implore you on behalf of Christ, be reconciled to God" (2 Cor. 5:20).

Peace Realized through Christ's Resurrection

Christ's death makes peace possible not only between man and God, but also among men. Yet Jesus did not merely die; he also rose from the grave, and it is his resurrection that actually creates peace. This is why we must always hold the cross and the open tomb together. Christ's death removes God's barriers to our acceptance, but it is the spiritual resurrection that takes place within us, as an outworking of Christ's resurrection, that changes us and brings us to God. It is by the Holy Spirit that we are, as Paul expresses it in Ephesians 2:5, "made . . . alive together with Christ." Now, Paul adds, by the power of his resurrection Christ has created "in himself one new man in place of the two, so making peace" (Eph. 2:15).

Paul says that in making us his disciples, Jesus created a new humanity and made us part of it. We are the people of his resurrection life, partaking of his power and joining the family of God. Jesus does not make peace by persuading two different types of people to get along for a while. He does not say to the Gentiles that they must be kind to Jews, and vice versa. He says, "You are no longer what you were. Do not think of yourself as a Jew any longer or as a Gentile any longer. Think of yourself as a Christian, a new kind of person." This viewpoint is especially important today: we are no longer white or black, rich or poor, Northern or Southern—we are Christians. Christianity is not a Band-Aid on the old humanity, with all its conflict and division. Christianity is a new humanity in Christ, in his resurrection, a humanity that has passed through the death of the cross and through the open tomb of the resurrection to receive eternal life.

What is it that makes us members of this new humanity? The answer is, of course, the new birth, which is what happens when someone believes in Jesus: "If anyone is in Christ, he is a new creation. The old has passed away; behold, the new has come" (2 Cor. 5:17). This is Paul's point in Ephesians as well—that in Christ we are something new; Christ died and rose again, that he "might reconcile us both to God in one body through the cross, thereby killing the hostility." Jesus brings us to God in such a way that he also brings us to one another. He gives us a new life and a new identity, which we now share with all our brothers and sisters in him.

This is the most radical way of making peace, by actually making us one. Our closest analogy is to be part of a natural family. We say that blood is thicker than water. Family members stick together and help one another, even when they don't get along. How much thicker yet is the bond of the Spirit. Jesus makes us one by giving each of us the same Spirit, bringing all of us into God's family and making us brothers and sisters for all eternity. This is the true basis for Christian unity: our mutual relationship to God, our mutual love for Christ, and our mutual indwelling by the same Holy Spirit so that we experience a spiritual oneness in Christ.

Peace Experienced in the New Humanity in Christ

This unity tells us what the church is: one new man in Jesus Christ, the new humanity that will live forever and partake in Christ's glory throughout all ages. This is why reflecting on Paul's message in Ephesians will remind us of the significance of the Christian church. There is nothing else like it, nothing else more important, and nothing else more worthy of our commitment, sacrifice, and contribution. We are not a social club, not a self-help society. We are the new creation brought about by the Spirit of God through the resurrection of Christ, the holy society of heaven living in this present evil world.

Do you see why it is so important that we should love the church? Do you see why it is so vital that we pursue holiness with a passion? The church is the bride of Christ, the new humanity of the resurrection! Angels gaze on us even now in wonder. Do you see why it is so important to be a part of the church? Only the church can know the peace of God, because it is in the church that Christ is making peace, through faith in him.

God sent Jesus to reconcile sinners to himself "in one body through the cross, thereby killing the hostility" (Eph. 2:16). So if you want to be part of this new humanity, you must come to the cross. This is Paul's logic in the second half of Ephesians 2: "But now in Christ Jesus you who once were far off have been brought near by the blood of Christ . . . , that he might create in himself one new man in place of the two, so making peace" (vv. 13–15). To be part of Christ's church you must enter through the cross, and having come to the cross you must enter into Christ's church, the resurrection humanity where Christ reigns in peace.

One of the great signs of assurance of salvation is to experience this unity and peace. Have you ever encountered someone with whom you would have no natural reason for friendship? But he or she is a Christian. You begin to talk about our Savior. God's Word enters your conversation, and your hearts are drawn together. That is a strong sign of God's Spirit dwelling in your life. And it causes the world to marvel, that in Christ we transcend every division that the world knows and that the world cannot overcome—racial, national, economic, occupational—and in Christ enjoy a spiritual union bathed in love.

Paul's description of the church has the most profound implications for our approach to ministry. We are told today that people like to be with others just like themselves. Church marketing experts tell us that if we pick out one kind of person and focus on their preferences, they will flock to the church and others who are like them will follow.[1] The result is one church for hip young white people, another for black people, another for Hispanics; one for the intellectuals, another for the emotionally needy; one for the outgoing and another for the reserved. The church today has become a sort of multiplex movie theater. Many a church even divides its own congregation with one service that is liturgical, another that is traditional, and another that is rock 'n' roll. It is a brilliantly successful approach—if numbers are what really matters.

But Paul emphasizes that the church is to be one new man in Christ. Christ wants to bring together otherwise hostile groups into one new body. Christ is not glorified when people get together on the basis of human divisions or preferences. The world does that. What glorifies Christ is to find all different kinds of people together because of their spiritual bond in Christ. We want young and old, single and married, hip and square, rich and poor together, from every tribe and race. How is this possible? Only by the Spirit of God, uniting in Christ people who would otherwise have nothing to do with each other.

To a certain extent a particular church is bound to have a particular cultural feel, simply because it has a history. But an overarching Christian culture transcends all of that. Worship should not be determined by cultural tradition, but should be shaped by the Bible as much as possible. We should mainly do things that Christians of all generations would recognize as distinctively Christian: confessing our sin and hearing God's pardon, proclaiming the creed, reading Scripture, praying, singing psalms, hymns, and spiritual songs (Col. 3:16), preaching the Word, receiving the sacraments. As we mature as believers, we increasingly love those things that are biblical and care less for those things of our cultural background. We are people of the new in Christ, and not of the old of the world.

United in Christ

We conclude with three observations that flow from this text. The first has to do with the kind of peace that God is making in this world. It is an inward peace, a peace of love and harmony and fellowship. It is not merely the cessation of fighting or arguing, and Christians should never settle for that.

So do you know the kind of peace that Paul is talking about? Is it found in your home, in your relationships at work, in your marriage? It is not always possible for us to enjoy the kind of peace we desire when it comes to non-Christians. Paul says in Romans 12:18, "So far as it depends on you, live peaceably with all." But in our relationships with Christians, and especially in our homes, we should experience this peace. It happens as we walk with God by the power of his Spirit and under the authority of his Word. Paul exhorts us in Colossians 3:15–16, "Let the peace of Christ rule in your hearts, to which indeed you were called in one body. And be thankful. Let the word of Christ dwell in you richly."

So why do many Christians know so little of this peace? I think it is because we do not realize all that is possible in the normal Christian life. I think it is because we do not know how willing and how able God is to answer our prayers with a supernatural work in our lives. Most Christians live as close to the world as they can and are under its influence, instead of living close to God and under his influence. We are to be in the world, but not of it. We lack peace because we lack holiness, that is, the renewing work of the Holy Spirit that turns our hearts to God. We do not take seriously the words of our Lord, "Peace I leave with you; my peace I give to you" (John 14:27).

Second, this passage should transform our idea of what the church is. The church is not just a building or an institution. The church is a new human race, the eternal family of God's people, whose work will endure long after every merely human achievement has fallen into dust. It is in the church that God is displaying his glory (Eph. 3:10), so God calls his people to serve for the building up of the church (4:12). You are called to use your gifts, contribute your time and money, offer your prayers and your tears, for the blessing and growth of the church, the new humanity in Christ.

Since Jesus bought the church with his blood in order to make peace, we should all loathe to disturb this peace and to bring division or conflict into the church. Apart from false teaching, nothing hurts a church more than division and conflict. So if we are part of a faithful, biblical church, then we should do everything possible to seek the purity and peace of the church. God forbid that any of us should disturb the peace of Christ's church, which he purchased with his precious blood.

Finally, this passage gives us a whole new perspective on the glory of Christ's saving work. We tend to think only about what Jesus does for us as individuals. But here we see a vast and grand panorama. Christ has overthrown the devil's work in the world. He has formed a new people for himself: a new race that transcends all the old conflicts, a new kingdom that overwhelms former allegiances and hostilities. Christ has not merely made some repairs to the old broken-down humanity. He has made something glorious and new in its place, using the raw materials of the fallen creation, cleansing us from sin and breathing into us the new life of his resurrection, thus making peace. This is where God's plan for history is heading, the fallen creation redeemed and restored in Christ: "The wolf shall dwell with the lamb, and the leopard shall lie down with the young goat, and the calf and the lion and the fattened calf together. . . . They shall not hurt or destroy in all my holy mountain; for the earth shall be full of the knowledge of the LORD as the waters cover the sea" (Isa. 11:6, 9).

This is our reality in Christ, and it is our future in Christ. As we trust in him and seek his peace, this resurrection reality will be our present experience in increasing measure, to our great blessing and to the glory of the grace of God.

Questions for Study and Reflection

1. How has God's judgment at the Tower of Babel (Gen. 11) shaped subsequent human history? What are some of the problems we each face as a result?
2. How did Pentecost respond to the Tower of Babel, and what does this tell us about God's redeeming purposes for our world?
3. The author states that true peace is made possible only by Christ's death for sin. Is this true? If so, why? What does this then say to us about the mission and ministry of Christians today?
4. What is legalism? Is it legalistic for Christians to emphasize obedience to God's commands? Are Christians able to obey God's law, if imperfectly? If so, by what power?
5. If peace is made possible by the crucifixion of Christ, how is it realized among believers through Christ's resurrection? How does this teaching affect your attitude towards your own Christian life?
6. Why is the church a "new humanity" in Christ, and why is it that God's peace is realized only here? If the church is God's agency for peace in this world, what kind of peace is it, and what does this say about the mission of the church in the world?

13

Access to the Father

Ephesians 2:17–18

And he came and preached peace to you who were far off and peace to those who were near. For through him we both have access in one Spirit to the Father.
—Ephesians 2:17–18

All through Ephesians, Paul addresses a question that is at the heart of his message: "What makes someone a Christian?" How does this happen? And in what does it result?

The first and most basic answer came in Ephesians 1:1, where Paul said that Christians are "saints"—that is, "holy ones"—through faith in Christ Jesus. By the time chapter 1 concluded, we had learned that a Christian is one who is beloved of God the Father (1:4–5), forgiven through the blood of Christ

(1:7), and indwelt by the Holy Spirit (1:13). In chapter 2, Paul added that a Christian is a sinner saved by grace, through faith, for the display of God's glory. Now, as we continue in chapter 2, we find another answer to the question, "What is a Christian?" Here, we find that a Christian is a person who has peace with God through the atoning blood of Jesus Christ, and experiences the peace of God that Jesus works into our hearts. For, as Paul exclaims, "he himself is our peace" (Eph. 2:14).

He Preached Peace

As Paul explains it, the peace that believers have with and from God results from the saving work of Christ. Starting in verse 13, Paul has explained that Jesus died in our place to give us peace with God through the forgiveness of our sins. He then rose from the grave and ascended into heaven to pour his peace into our hearts through the Holy Spirit. Now, in verse 17, Paul notes one more thing that Jesus has done to give us peace: "He came and preached peace to you who were far off and peace to those who were near."

This is a remarkable statement, especially when we consider it in the order in which Paul puts it. We might think that when Paul speaks of Jesus' preaching peace he is referring to Jesus' earthly ministry, when he went about teaching and healing. But it is clear from the placement in Paul's teaching that he does not in fact mean this. Jesus first died, then rose from the grave, and then preached peace. Also, we note that Jesus preached peace to those who were both far off and near, meaning to both Gentiles and Jews. The Gospels reveal that this did not happen during the three years of Jesus' earthly ministry.

Paul is therefore speaking of the time of the apostles, when the gospel went out to the Gentiles, when the Holy Spirit inspired the writing of the New Testament books, and when men such as Paul went about preaching good news. This was,

Paul says, the continued work of Jesus Christ as he proclaimed peace through his apostles.

This idea comes across clearly in Acts 1:8, where Jesus spoke to his disciples just before he ascended into heaven. "You will receive power when the Holy Spirit has come upon you," he said, "and you will be my witnesses in Jerusalem and in all Judea and Samaria, and to the end of the earth." This means that when the apostles preached, Jesus was preaching through them. When they wrote the New Testament, Jesus was writing to us through them. This principle holds true even today, when a minister faithfully preaches Christ's gospel or when a faithful Christian shares the good news from God's Word. It is Jesus himself who is preaching, offering peace to sinners who are alienated from God, peace to the brokenhearted and fearful, and peace from God to a world gripped in conflict and sorrow.

It is with the same love that bore our sins on the cross that Jesus speaks today through his Word. The love in his heart for the lost and the needy has not burned out one bit. No less than when he cleansed the leper or forgave the woman caught in adultery, no less than when he multiplied the few pieces of fish and bread to feed the hungry crowds, Jesus looks upon you now with compassion, mercy, and the great love of God. He preaches good news of peace to you: peace with God, peace in your own heart, and peace on earth through the gospel of his grace. It is a peace he can offer because he purchased it with his own blood; a peace he can truly give because of the Holy Spirit he sends to all who believe; and a peace he preaches to you because of the mercy and grace that still beats within his heart as he reigns in heaven and prepares for his return.

Access to the Father

A second thing that stands out in these two verses is the clear evidence that Paul wants Christians to understand salvation and our relationship to God in terms of the doctrine of the Trinity. This is something that is distinctive to Christians: we do not relate merely to God in the abstract but to the three persons of the Godhead. When we speak of having a "personal relationship with God," it is because of what the Bible reveals about the persons of the Trinity. Few passages in the New Testament present this truth as clearly as does verse 18. Paul writes, "For through him [that is, Christ] we both have access in one Spirit to the Father."

The doctrine of the Trinity is not just something for scholars to rack their brains on. Trinity is who God is. So if we are to know God and relate to God, we must think about God as Trinity. We are living in a time when the Trinity is forgotten by many Christians. Some Christians think about Jesus only. Their worship is directed only to God the Son, and their salvation is founded only on what he does and gives. Yet that is not what even Jesus intends. Other Christians focus all their attention on the Spirit and his power. But the New Testament emphasizes our relationship to the whole Trinity: Father, Son, and Holy Spirit.

This is obviously important to Paul. In Ephesians 1:3–14, he worked out the blessings of salvation in terms of the Trinity. If we want to know and have all the blessings that Christianity offers, then we must know all three persons of the Trinity. Now in Ephesians 2:18, he applies this to our relationship to God. Our salvation involves and depends on all three members of the Trinity.

In this way, Paul wraps up his teaching on the peace made available to us through Jesus Christ. First, he makes the great statement that through Christ "we . . . have access . . . to the Father." This means that Jesus came into this world and died on the cross, not merely to bring us into relationship with himself, but most specifically to bring us into a relationship of love with God the Father.

This purpose of Jesus comes through in many places, but perhaps best in his prayer to the Father on the night of his arrest. In John 17:4, Jesus prays, "I glorified you on earth, having accomplished the work that you gave me to do." As Jesus goes on to say, that work was to reveal the Father and bring his people into a saving relationship with the Father. Similarly, when Jesus said in John 14:6, "I am the way, and the truth, and the life," it was in answer to Thomas's question about how the disciples could know God the Father and enter into his blessing.

Therefore, Christianity's aim is that people who have been separated from God's love would now come to the heavenly Father and enter into the light of his presence as beloved children. We are adopted into the family of God the Father, through the saving work of God the Son, by the ministry of God the Holy Spirit.

This makes an important point that is of vast importance to our lives. So many people, even Christians, feel good about Jesus but think of God the Father as a threatening, disapproving, and hostile force lurking in the background. The result is that they never enjoy the peace that Jesus came to give. God the Father is seen as an angry judge, and you know that you really haven't lived up to his demands. God the Father is holy and perfect, and you aren't holy and perfect. You don't pray as you should. You haven't broken away from your sins the way you should. So you feel distant from God. You wonder whether the promises of the Bible are really for you because you don't measure up.

If you feel this way, the gospel Christ preaches has two things to say to you. The first is that Jesus does not cajole a reluctant, grumpy, or unwilling Father to look on you in love. Rather, the Father himself sent Jesus into the world because of his love for you. John 3:16 proclaims, "For God so loved the world, that he gave his only Son." Paul states in Ephesians 1:4–5, "In love [God] predestined us for adoption as sons through Jesus Christ." If you trust in Christ, you can know that the heavenly Father loved you before you were even born, before the worlds came into existence. He knew you by name and wanted your heart to know his love. This is why Jesus came into the world—not to persuade a reluctant, angry God about you, but to serve a God of love by taking away your sin and making you a child of the Father.

But what about your unworthiness? What about the truth that you don't pray as you should, that you forget about God much of the time, and that you don't measure up to him? How can a holy God love you? The answer is found in the gospel that Jesus came and preached. The gospel says that everything that needs to happen to open the way for the holy Father to pour his love on you was accomplished by Jesus Christ. You must be righteous to stand in God's presence, and Jesus fulfilled the law for you and grants to you by faith an imputed righteousness that is perfect in God's sight (see 2 Cor. 5:21).

But you say, "My sin and guilt makes me unclean before God, and I feel nervous thinking about him." The gospel replies that Jesus shed his blood to cleanse you once and for all before God. Ephesians 2:13 says, "Now in Christ Jesus you who once were far off have been brought near by the blood of Christ." The apostle John adds, "If we confess our sins, he is faithful and just to forgive us our sins and to cleanse us from all unrighteousness" (1 John 1:9).

But you don't know where your heart will be tomorrow. Who knows whether you will remain faithful to God? The book of Hebrews reminds you that Jesus now lives and reigns in heaven, praying for you, ensuring the Holy Spirit's ministry in your life. Hebrews 7:25 explains, "Consequently, he is able to save to the uttermost those who draw near to God through him, since he always lives to make intercession for them."

Understanding Christ's work for you to achieve God the Father's own purpose of love will change your life. It will cast away darkness with light. As Martyn Lloyd-Jones describes it: "I am no longer filled with a craven fear of God. He is no longer to me some tyrant waiting to pounce on me and to damn me and to hurl me to hell. He is my loving Father who loved me with an everlasting love, with such a love as to send His only Son to die on the Cross for me. And the moment I realize that, I am at peace with Him."[1]

Therefore, Jesus' desire, the reason he died and the cause for which he presently reigns, is for us to draw near to God the Father through him. He wants us to know the Father's love, which fulfills the deepest needs of our hearts. What do we gain from a father? We gain our identity, our name, from our father. This is what God will do for you. He will take you as his own child. We gain acceptance from our earthly fathers, and God wants to give his acceptance to you. Fathers grant provision and protection and security, and God the Father wants to give you a destiny and an inheritance in glory. He will take care of you. These are the things that a father gives, and God the Father will give them to you through Jesus Christ.

Not a few people have a hard time turning to God as Father because of the painful experiences they have had with their earthly fathers. They were not accepted but were rejected. They received not care but abuse. Their father's discipline tore them down instead of building them up. But if you were let down by your earthly father in those ways or others, do not turn away from God the Father. Turn to him. He is the good and perfect Father. All that you ever longed for, and that earthly fathers sometimes fail to give, God the Father wants to give for the blessing of your heart.

Paul teaches that through Jesus all Christians, both Jews and Gentiles, have "access . . . to the Father." The idea is more than that God is available to us, but that God invites us into his love. God delights to see his children because we are forgiven in Christ and clothed in his perfect righteousness. We should never fear to draw near to God, because through Jesus Christ we have access.

I recently read an article about old-fashioned courting practices that reminded me of this principle. Back in the days when young men came to call at young ladies' homes, and the courting took place in the parlor, it was the women who initiated the relationship. Without an invitation it was considered rude for a man to show up at a young lady's home or to initiate personal contact. Without an invitation he would be turned away at the door if he came.

That is the way it is with God. If you show up at heaven's gate without an invitation, you will be turned away. God is holy and his heaven is holy, and those stained by sin—even "respectable" sin—will certainly be turned away. So God sent his Son into the world to grant an invitation—to give access—to those who believe in him. And if you are in Christ, then you have a permanent invitation into God's affections. He sees you clothed in perfect white, with all your stains removed by Christ's precious blood, and you are welcome with him.

Jesus wants you to have this relationship with the Father, and the Spirit's work is to empower you for it. We have "access in one Spirit to the Father." This is what makes us one in Christ, that we all have equal access by the same Spirit. The Spirit does not want us focusing on himself. "He will glorify me," Jesus said (John 16:14), and Jesus is glorified when sinners come to the Father in faith.

Thus, our salvation is tightly woven in the combined work of the three divine persons of the Trinity. You are saved because God the Father loves you, because God the Son gained your access by the cross, and because God the Spirit is working in your heart to bring you to God. This is the pattern and structure of our whole salvation: we are saved to the Father, through the Son, by the Holy Spirit.

Praying to the Father

I want to apply this Trinitarian pattern directly to the matter of prayer. Ephesians 2:18 is one of the most important verses in the Bible when it comes to prayer. It tells us how prayer "works."

Most of us struggle with prayer because we do not understand what Paul teaches here. Our approach is what I like to call

The Wizard of Oz model of prayer. In that well-known movie, a girl named Dorothy from Kansas is transported into the magical land of Oz. She wants to go home and is told to seek out the great and powerful Wizard of Oz, who lives in the Emerald City. As she travels there, she is joined by the Scarecrow, who wants a brain, the Tin Woodman, who needs a heart, and the Cowardly Lion, who is shamed by his lack of courage.

After some adventures, the little band arrives at the Emerald City and asks to see the Wizard. They are told what many of us expect to be told about God: he is too busy for such puny people; they have no right to intrude on the great and powerful Oz. But with daring and resourcefulness, Dorothy manages to get into the chamber to see the Wizard. He is ominous and scary; his face is wreathed in flames and smoke. Fearfully, she makes her requests, but the Wizard refuses to grant them. She must first complete a quest to prove her worth. It is only after she succeeds and returns with the broomstick of the Wicked Witch of the West that the Wizard is willing to help, after which we learn that he is not really so great and powerful after all.

That is how many of us think about prayer. God is too busy, and our prayers are a bother. Even if we get his attention, we face a daunting, unwilling deity. If God does answer our prayers, it is only because we have first done something for him or otherwise won his favor, so that we are pretty much on our own. With all that, why bother to pray?

But what Paul writes here totally changes our view of God and of prayer. It is true that God is great and powerful, but he also knows and loves you. He did not wait in his distant chamber for you to come, but sent his Son into your world. It is true that your sins stand against you and that the devil opposes you, the way the Wicked Witch tried to stop Dorothy. But God's Son removed your sin and defeated the devil on the cross. He presents his own achievement for you to the Father, who is glad to receive you and happy to care for you, who responds to your prayers with his love and grants you his peace (Phil. 4:7, 19). The Scarecrow wanted a brain, and God will give you a right mind and a knowledge of truth; the Tin Woodman wanted a heart, and God will plant a new heart within you, one that longs to do his will; the Cowardly Lion wanted courage, and God will strengthen you against fear. Dorothy wanted to go home, and God has prepared a home for you and will strengthen you as you journey through this life.

Returning to verse 18, we ask, "Why will God answer our prayers?" The answer is that we have "access . . . to the Father." Jesus is in heaven, hand-delivering all our prayers with hands that were pierced by nails for you. This is why we pray, "In Jesus' name"; that is what we mean when we end our prayers that way. We are asking Jesus to be the mailman who delivers our prayers to God, and we are thereby certain that they will arrive and be received with loving care.

How can people like us actually pray and talk to God in a right way? Paul tells us that it is by the Spirit. In Romans 8:26, Paul says of prayer, "The Spirit helps us in our weakness." He enters into our prayers and sorts them out before God. Paul adds, "The Spirit intercedes for the saints according to the will of God" (8:27).

It makes a tremendous difference to understand how the three persons of the Trinity work together to enable us to pray. But most importantly, Paul reminds us that we have a heavenly Father who invites us to pray. Philip Graham Ryken says, "A real father is a man who has a passionate love for his family. Because of the warmth of his affection . . . his children have confidence to ask him for what they need."[2] Surely that is why, when his disciples asked, Jesus told them to come to God in prayer, saying, "Our Father which art in heaven" (Matt. 6:9 KJV).

How Beautiful Are the Feet

We conclude with three observations. The first is for those who have never trusted in Christ. This is what you are missing if your heart is closed to Jesus. The good news that Paul writes of in this chapter is the best you could possibly hear. It is good news for your eternal destiny and for your life on this earth, if you will believe. Jesus came to bring sinners near to God through his blood (Eph. 2:13). He came to be our peace (2:14). He gives us access into the love of the heavenly Father through his blood and by the ministry of the Holy Spirit. Why will you stand far off from that? Paul says in verse 17 that even as you read this, it is Jesus himself, with all the love of God in his heart, who preaches good news of peace to you. As Paul elsewhere said, "In Christ God was reconciling the world to himself, not counting their trespasses against them, and entrusting to us the message of reconciliation. Therefore, we are ambassadors for Christ, God making his appeal through us. We implore you on behalf of Christ, be reconciled to God" (2 Cor. 5:19–20). You can call on God right now through faith in Jesus Christ, and you will be saved.

Second, if you have believed in Christ, then realize all that he has achieved for you according to God's own plan. You have access to God the Father, a permanent invitation into his love and a place in his heart forever. If that is true, then live in the light of God's love. Do not let feelings of guilt or inadequacy keep you from God, but let them remind you how precious is the blood of Christ and how amazing is the grace that draws you near. Martyn Lloyd-Jones observes:

> The moment you see that you are made righteous by Christ and clothed in His righteousness, you can go to God with confidence. He is your Father, He is waiting to receive you and you can pray as you have never prayed before. The way is clear, it is a new and a living way that has been opened. You are at peace with God and at peace within; you have found rest for your soul.[3]

Finally, if we believe this news and know it in our lives, then surely we will tell others. Paul says that Jesus came and preached good news of peace; we know from the Great Commission that he wants us to go and do the same (Matt. 28:18–20). Once you know the reality of God's love for you, he will give you love for others and cause you to preach good news of peace so that they, too, might have access to the Father, through the Son, by the Spirit. And then what Isaiah said about our Lord Jesus will be true of you as well: "How beautiful upon the mountains are the feet of him who brings good news, who publishes peace" (Isa. 52:7).

Questions for Study and Reflection

1. What are some of the biblical descriptions of a Christian? How are these all important?
2. The author states that when Paul says Christ "preached peace," he refers not to Christ's earthly ministry, but to his present heavenly ministry. How can Christ be preaching today, when he is in heaven?
3. Why is it vital for Christians to understand their salvation in terms of the whole Trinity? What is the danger if we focus only on one Person of the Trinity? How do the Father, Son, and Holy Spirit work together in our salvation?
4. When Jesus died on the cross, was he changing the Father's mind about us? Why do some people think this way? What difference does it make to realize that Jesus was doing the Father's will in reconciling us to God?
5. What does the author mean by the *Wizard of Oz* model of prayer? Have you experienced this? How does Christ's atoning blood give us access to the Father in prayer? What is the biblical model of prayer and how do you find that it helps your spiritual life?

14

Citizens and Children

Ephesians 2:19

So then you are no longer strangers and aliens, but you are fellow citizens with the saints and members of the household of God.
—Ephesians 2:19

In 1962, William Edgar arrived as a seventeen-year-old freshman at Harvard University. As he tells it, his life was focused on a trinity that consisted of soccer, French existential philosophy, and jazz piano. As he recounts in *Finding God at Harvard*, Edgar's freshman year was humbling: he found others who were better at soccer and piano and few who cared about his philosophy. By his sophomore year he was starting to adjust, when he took a survey course in Western literature. As often happens in universities, this class had one large lecture with the professor and then smaller discussion classes with teaching assistants. Edgar's teaching assistant was an articulate Christian named Harold O. J. Brown, who would go on to be one of the great theology professors of our time. Through Brown's Christian critique of literature and personal discussions outside of class, Edgar was introduced to a new Trinity: Father, Son, and Holy Spirit. On his teacher's advice, he spent his sophomore summer at the Swiss Christian community L'Abri with the renowned apologist Francis Schaeffer. When Edgar returned to Harvard for his junior year, it was as a committed Christian.

Edgar's return to Harvard involved considerable change for him. He mainly remembered that everything seemed new and alive because he was alive to God. He abandoned his unbelieving philosophy. He regained his love for soccer, no longer needing to be the best but only to do his best. His music was especially impacted, and he sought out the Christian spirituality beneath much of the jazz music he loved. As many other college-age converts have found, perhaps the most challenging changes were social. "Some of my friends thought I had become a little strange!" he remembers. "Though they did not exactly abandon me, I felt they were studying me. More challenging still, in my newfound faith I felt obliged to seek out other Christians."[1]

Aliens No More

Edgar's experience is completely consistent with Paul's explanation of Christian salvation in Ephesians chapter 2. Ephesians 2:1–10 says that we begin as sinners who are saved in a spiritual resurrection by God's grace, through faith in Christ. The second half of chapter 2 looks at salvation from a more corporate perspective. Starting in verse 12, Paul reminds us that apart from Christ we were aliens to God's people and covenant, therefore "having no hope and without God in the world." When we trust in Christ and are saved, we not only become new individuals who enter into new relationships. We also become citizens of God's kingdom together with the saints, we become children together with brothers and sisters in God's household, and we become part of a building, a living temple, in which God lives in the Spirit. All these results flow to us in Jesus Christ, and we enjoy them with all other believers.

In this chapter we will look at the first two of these new relationships brought about by Christ, starting with *citizenship in God's kingdom.* Paul writes, "So then you are no longer strangers and aliens, but you are fellow citizens with the saints." God rules over an eternal kingdom, and having come to God through faith in Christ, we are no longer aliens to it but citizens of it.

Paul uses two words here to describe our former condition, the first of which is "strangers," people who belong somewhere else but are traveling through. The second word, "aliens," describes resident foreigners. These are people living among us who hold their citizenship elsewhere.

We all know what it is like to be outsiders, to not fit in or understand the place where we are. We often experience this feeling when we are traveling in a different country. We don't know the language or the culture. The food is strange, and the people act in ways we don't understand. Furthermore, strangers are treated with suspicion; aliens are not made to feel welcome because their loyalties are different. They don't belong, and their presence makes people feel uncomfortable. Undoubtedly, this is how many foreign residents feel about living in the United States. Their status is insecure, and much that they experience is unfamiliar and threatening. Strangers and aliens long for a home, for acceptance and belonging.

Like it or not, this is what Paul says was true about his Gentile readers before they came to faith in Christ. They were not part of God's kingdom. He has used forms of these very terms in verse 12, saying that they were "alienated from the commonwealth of Israel and strangers to the covenants of promise." God was in the world and he had a people, but they weren't part of that select group. The fellowship of God and his people was strange and unfamiliar, and they had no right to claim a place within it. Unsaved people feel the same today. Even when Christians try to be friendly, unbelievers often don't feel comfortable. Their hearts were created for the worship of God, but they don't know how. They long for truth, but they find God's Word strange and offensive to their sinful nature. They need God in their lives, but they don't know how to pray.

This is how it was for Paul's Gentile readers before he came to Ephesus with the gospel. Before that time, they groped around in pagan idolatry, trying in futility to relate to God. So God sent his own Son into the world to make peace with men by dying on the cross. Through Jesus' resurrection God sent new life into the world, and through the apostles Christ preached his peace. The result was a great change for those who heard and believed; through faith in Christ they became "fellow citizens with the saints."

In our day, the privilege of citizenship means sharing in the cause of your country and being allowed to vote. This is similar to what happens to us when we join the church: we take up its cause and have a right to participate in ministry. In Paul's time, a bit more was involved in citizenship: citizens had a right to protection that noncitizens did not have. Once, when a mob rose against him in Jerusalem and the Roman commander was going to have him beaten, Paul revealed that he was a Roman citizen. Immediately the whips were put away and the soldiers protected him. His citizenship granted him the right to appeal to Caesar for justice; in fact, it was while Paul was waiting for this audience in Rome that he wrote his letter to the Ephesians.

Likewise, being a citizen allows us to benefit from God's kingdom. The Romans enjoyed provision, protection, fair government, and justice. In America, our citizenship secures for us freedom from unlawful seizure and freedom to make a living. What, then, are the benefits of citizenship in God's kingdom? Our main benefits are spelled out in the new covenant promise, found in Jeremiah 31:3–34 and recalled in Hebrews 8:8–12, where God declares, "I will put my laws into their minds, and write them on their hearts, and I will be their God, and they shall be my people. . . . I will be merciful toward their iniquities, and I will remember their sins no more." We might think of these benefits in terms of the three tenses of our salvation: the past tense—justification; the present tense—sanctification; and the future tense—glorification. These are rights that believers gain as citizens of God's kingdom.

In the Sermon on the Mount, Jesus spoke of his Father's watching over every hair on our heads, so that citizenship in God's kingdom gives us freedom from anxiety. Our citizenship means having the Good Shepherd, Jesus Christ, to rule in us by his love. The Westminster Shorter Catechism says that Jesus executes his office of king "in subduing us to himself, in ruling and defending us, and in restraining and conquering all his and our enemies" (A. 26). The Bible often describes God's kingdom in terms of a great city-state, so we can rejoice at Psalm 46's description of the gospel's flowing through that city, giving life and peace and joy to all who drink from its waters: "There is a river whose streams make glad the city of God. . . . God is in the midst of her; she shall not be moved" (Ps. 46:4–5).

With these blessings come obligations. The Shorter Catechism addresses this principle simply. In answer to the question, "What is the duty which God requireth of man?" it says, "The duty which God requireth of man, is obedience to his revealed will" (Q. 39). We are to trust God, love God, and serve God, all of which find expression through obedience to the Word of God in the Bible.

When Paul writes of our citizenship in God's kingdom, we should remember where he was at that moment. Paul was in Rome, either in prison or under house arrest. All around him were the great buildings that were a monument to empire. Roman citizenship was the most prized possession one could have. If one did not receive it by birth—and only a few did—then it could be purchased only at great cost. Paul was a Roman citizen, having been raised in the Roman city of Tarsus. But that was not his glory. That was not his source of pride, hope, or confidence. "Our citizenship is in heaven," he boasted (Phil. 3:20). And as he writes from Rome to these Ephesian Christians, he wants that to be their glory as well.

Imagine Paul saying such a thing to the average Roman of his day. To a Roman, immortality was gained through participation in the greatness of Rome. And here was Paul, throwing all that away for the kingdom of a Galilean Messiah. To be a Christian always involves a clash of kingdoms—the kingdoms of this world and the kingdom of God and of Christ. This conflict came through most vividly at Jesus' trial. Pontius Pilate scoffed at the idea of Jesus' being a king. Jesus did not have any of the accoutrements. He had no army, no treasury, no badge of office. "So you are a king?" Pilate scoffed, in response to Jesus' assertion, "My kingdom is not from the world" (John 18:36–37).

Jesus' kingdom is heavenly and not earthly. That does not make it inferior, but superior. Above all the kingdoms of earth is Christ's heavenly kingdom. While the Caesars rule over the body, Jesus rules over the soul; while worldly kings may rule affairs in this life, Christ rules over eternity. That is why Paul was no longer impressed by the glory of the Roman empire, and why he gloried only in the kingdom of God in which he had citizenship through faith in Christ.

Verse 19 shows one of the differences between worldly kingdoms and the kingdom of Christ. Paul says, "You are fellow citizens with the saints." This speaks of the character of God's kingdom in which we are made citizens, in comparison with that of the world. God's kingdom is one of peace, love, and harmony. It is a holy kingdom, in which everyone who joins becomes one with the saints. That word "saints" refers not to a few super-spiritual giants, but to all the people of God, those made holy by the blood of Christ. Ours is a kingdom of holy union, holy love, and holy purpose. James Montgomery Boice observes the difference between God's kingdom and the Roman empire that held Paul captive:

> When Paul wrote these words the kingdom of Rome was at the height of its territorial expansion and glory. Rome dominated the world. Roman armies kept peace and dispensed justice. Roman roads linked the far-flung reaches of the Empire. Rome had stood for hundreds of years and was thought to be able to stand for thousands of years more. But Paul looked at Rome and saw it, not as one great united Kingdom, but as a force imposed on mutually antagonistic factions: rich and poor, free man and slave, man and woman, Jew and Gentile. And in its place he saw this new humanity, created by God himself, transcending these boundaries. This kingdom was destined to grow and permeate all nations, drawing from all peoples. It is a kingdom that cannot be shaken or destroyed.[2]

Where is the Roman empire today? Where are the many other empires that have risen and fallen since Paul's time? What is the destiny of every worldly kingdom, but to come and go as God desires? As the apostle John puts it, "The world is passing away along with its desires, but whoever does the will of God abides forever" (1 John 2:17).

Paul realized this dichotomy as he wrote from his prison cell in Rome. If he would only renounce Christ, or even back off from preaching the gospel, just fitting into the world as it was, he could have kept all that his Roman citizenship offered him. But Paul saw with a keener vision the realities of faith. As he writes in 2 Corinthians 4:17, "This light momentary affliction is preparing for us an eternal weight of glory beyond all comparison."

Members of God's Household

Citizenship in God's kingdom is one result of our salvation in Christ. But Paul goes on to speak of another relationship that is more personal. We may be all members of the same country but not be members of the same family, so Paul is bringing us closer in when he adds: "and members of the household of God" (Eph. 2:19). Here is a relationship, and a unity with others, that is intimate and intense. Here we have gone from the legal relationship to the blood relationship. Just as blood unites a family, God's Spirit unites all believers as fellow members of his household.

This means, for one thing, that this relationship is only for those who are born again in Christ Jesus. Jesus said, in effect, "You must be born again to even see the kingdom of God" (John 3:3). That is because God's kingdom is also a family, and just as a family is defined by blood relations, God's household is bound by an inner, spiritual unity. People may like to believe that God is everyone's Father, but the Bible teaches that he is a Father only to those who are his children in Jesus Christ: "To all who did receive him, who believed in his name, he gave the right to become children of God, who were born, not of blood nor of the will of the flesh nor of the will of man, but of God" (John 1:12–13).

That God should make us members of his own household speaks volumes about his amazing love. It would be enough to praise God through all eternity if he simply refrained from condemning us as sinners. We deserve hell, and God forgives us through Jesus Christ. That alone is more than we could have ever imagined. Martyn Lloyd-Jones writes: "It would have been a wonderful thing if God had merely decided not to leave us in that state and not to punish us. But God's way of salvation does not stop at that. He elevates us to this dignity of children, He adopts us into His own family."[3]

Imagine appearing before an uncompromising judge for a crime that you most certainly did commit. All the evidence condemns you, and you have no defense. But just when your sentence is to be read, the judge tells you that he loves you and that his own son has agreed to serve your sentence, and that furthermore, he wants you to come home with him, to take his name and be his child, so that he may teach you to sin no more and that you may enter into fellowship with others who are beneficiaries of that same love. What would you say to that? You would marvel at his grace and give all the love in your heart to such a man. That is what God does in his love, and through the sacrifice of his Son you are now members of the household of God.

This is the love Jesus presented in his parable of the prodigal son. The son had fallen into sin and squandered his father's estate in sinful living. But when he repented and started home in disgrace, his father saw him coming from a long way off. Jesus tells what happened:

> While he was still a long way off, his father saw him and felt compassion, and ran and embraced him and kissed him. And the son said to him, "Father, I have sinned against heaven and before you. I am no longer worthy to be called your son." But the father said to his servants, "Bring quickly the best robe, and put it on him, and put a ring on his hand, and shoes on his feet. And

> bring the fattened calf and kill it, and let us eat and celebrate. For this my son was dead, and is alive again; he was lost, and is found." And they began to celebrate. (Luke 15:20–24)

If you have never come to God the Father through faith in Jesus Christ his Son, this is the love you are missing. This is the celebration that awaits every lost sinner who is a stranger and alien to the grace and salvation of God. God's people are a family that celebrates with great joy every sinner who is saved, and who are preparing now for an eternity together in the light of God's love.

If being a citizen of God's kingdom gives many benefits, how much greater are the benefits that flow from this more intimate familial relationship. A king must provide for his people, but how much more is a father concerned for his children. As children of God, we have the right to come to God in prayer and have him care for our needs. Jesus said, "Your Father knows what you need before you ask him" (Matt. 6:8). "If you then, who are evil, know how to give good gifts to your children, how much more will your Father who is in heaven give good things to those who ask him!" (7:11).

Wonderful as is God's fatherly care in this life, it is far surpassed by what awaits all his children in the life to come. In Romans 8:17, Paul writes that "if [we are] children, then [we are] heirs—heirs of God and fellow heirs with Christ, provided we suffer with him in order that we may also be glorified with him."

A Child of the King

If you put these two together—Paul's teaching that in Christ we are citizens of God's kingdom and children in God's family—then we are rightly described by the words of the hymn:

I once was an outcast stranger on earth,
a sinner by choice, and an alien by birth!
But I've been adopted, my name's written down,
an heir to a mansion, a robe, and a crown.
I'm a child of the King, a child of the King!
With Jesus, my Savior, I'm a child of the King.[4]

These lines express the great reality for everyone who trusts in Jesus Christ. We were strangers and aliens. We did not fit in, and we had no place in God's kingdom or his family. We had no real answer for the great problems of life, much less of eternity. Man in sin is estranged from God and from God's blessings. So God in his love sent Jesus Christ to be our peace, to reconcile us to God by suffering the punishment in our place, and to bring us into a real community with peace and love. If you are not a Christian, that is what God offers you through his Son, Jesus Christ.

If you are a Christian, then God wants you to know these privileges and blessings that are now your calling. The trouble with so many of our lives is that we do not understand the implications of what it means to be a Christian. We do not realize our position. From the perspective of heaven, during the eternity that is to come, we will be baffled by the attitude we so often now take, by our fixation on the things of earth, our doubting of God's faithful affection, and our lack of concern for the well-being of our brothers and sisters.

So often people think about what they have to give up if they become Christians. It certainly is true that following Christ will involve leaving former habits and relationships, and it certainly means turning away from sins we have loved. William Edgar discovered that truth when he came to Christ as a Harvard student. But he also learned that God was not narrowing his scope but vastly increasing it; God was making him a member of his glorious kingdom. God was not stripping him away from relationships where he belonged but entering him into his true home, introducing him to those who would truly love him and with whom he had real spiritual unity. Years later, when the class members returned to Harvard for their twenty-fifth reunion, Edgar had the privilege of preaching in the chapel about the blessings that flow from the death and resurrection of Christ, inviting his classmates to enter God's eternal kingdom for the salvation of their souls. In one of his books, Edgar said of the gospel, "To believe this message is to come home. Like the prodigal in Jesus' parable, we are homeless, lost in an alien land, until we come back home to the Father."[5]

Man was made by God and for God. We each have a God-shaped hole in our hearts that can be filled only by returning to him, by entering God's kingdom and joining his household as children. Until we do, we are restless, hungry, and thirsty for meaning and a place to belong. Through faith in Christ, God offers us nothing less than the fulfillment of these, our greatest and deepest needs. God sent his Son to save us from our sin. But forgiveness is just the beginning, not the end. Jesus Christ saves us to heavenly citizenship and to membership in a family where we belong. Edgar observed, "Much of our contemporary culture is alienated from God. The gospel calls it to come home."[6]

Only God, through Jesus Christ, can make life sacred, can give eternal meaning to our labor, and can offer us a home where we belong forever. When Christians realize that this is what we have, that this is what we are—royal children, princes and princesses in the kingdom and household of God—we will have all the motivation we need to live out the Christian life in accordance with God's Word. God simply calls us to be what he has made us in Christ: to serve faithfully in his kingdom and to love one another as brothers and sisters who share in his love.

Questions for Study and Reflection

1. What does Paul mean by referring to non-Christians as "aliens" and "strangers" to God? How has this changed through faith in Christ? What are some of our privileges as citizens in God's kingdom?
2. What does it say about God's love that he makes his enemies to be members of his own household? What does this tell us about God's purpose for us in salvation? How does this suggest that we should relate to God in Christ?
3. How might you use the two privileges Paul speaks of in this passage—citizenship in God's kingdom and membership in God's household—to explain Christianity to a non-believer?
4. How does our knowledge of God's blessings in Christ and our new identity as citizens and children motivate us to serve and glorify God?

15

A Holy Temple

Ephesians 2:20–22

. . . built on the foundation of the apostles and prophets, Christ Jesus himself being the cornerstone, in whom the whole structure, being joined together, grows into a holy temple in the Lord. In him you also are being built together into a dwelling place for God by the Spirit.
—Ephesians 2:20–22

I see a billboard from time to time that always makes me smile and think about our Lord Jesus. The billboard proclaims, "We Buy Ugly Houses." I suppose that slogan means that if your house is in bad shape and no one else will buy it, these people will take it off your hands, fix it up, and sell it at a profit. It is probably a good business, and one that may actually help people.

What makes me think about Jesus is that he does pretty much the same thing with us. Jesus is not like a prospective home-buyer who travels around with an agent, looking for the most attractive, most luxurious house, already all put together, at the least cost to himself. Instead, his motto might be akin to the one on the billboard: "I Buy Ugly Houses." Not only is that true, but Jesus also pays not the lowest cost possible but the highest price imaginable. The apostle Paul informs believers, "You were bought with a price" (1 Cor. 6:20), and Peter tells us, "You were ransomed . . . not with perishable things such as silver or gold, but with the precious blood of Christ" (1 Peter 1:18–19).

Jesus bought us not because we were so attractive or intelligent or good. What Paul wrote to the Corinthians is also true of us: "Not many of you were wise according to worldly standards, not many were powerful, not many were of noble birth" (1 Cor. 1:26). In fact, Jesus bought us, like ugly houses, when we were covered in the guilt and the filth of our sin. Romans 5:6–8 declares, "While we were still weak, at the right time Christ died for the ungodly. . . . God shows his love for us in that while we were still sinners, Christ died for us." That is the good news of Christianity. We are not saved because we are so attractive or worthy in any sense. We are saved because of the compassion and grace of a loving God in Jesus Christ. And the best news of all is not only that Jesus buys ugly houses, but that he fixes them up, and then fills them with his Spirit—houses in which God himself comes to live.

This is the teaching of the apostle Paul in this final passage of Ephesians 2. In Christ, he says, we are "a holy temple in the Lord . . . a dwelling place for God" (Eph. 2:21–22). This is both Paul's conclusion to his doctrine of salvation and the bridge he builds to his teaching on the church and the Christian life in the following chapters, which shows us that the church is nothing less than the outworking of Christ's saving work in individuals. Here, Paul tells us that the Christian church is built as the temple in which God will live forever; he describes the all-important foundation for the church; and he points to Christ himself as the cornerstone on which this temple rests.

A Holy Temple

The foundational point Paul makes is that the Christian church is built as a holy temple in which God will dwell. Unlike other buildings that are put together by bricks and mortar, this building is made up of God's people themselves and bound together by the Spirit of God. The apostle Peter teaches, "As you come to him [that is, Christ], a living stone rejected by men but in the sight of God chosen and precious, you yourselves like living stones are being built up as a spiritual house, to be a holy priesthood, to offer spiritual sacrifices acceptable to God through Jesus Christ" (1 Peter 2:4–5).

All through the latter half of Ephesians 2, Paul has had in mind the Jewish temple as a way of depicting the peace Christ gives. A veil separated sinful man from God, and Christ removed it by his death. There was a wall of division between Jew and Gentile, and that, too, is now gone.

Paul must have thought about the temple as he traveled throughout the ancient world, preaching and starting churches. Paul had many difficulties and disappointments, but his heart must have been thrilled to know that just as the stonemasons in Solomon's day had worked hard to fashion the great blocks to build that temple, he, too, was working hard to build a temple, one that would shine in glory forever.

The Bible's teaching on the temple begins with God's promise to David that his son would build God's house: "I will raise up your offspring after you, who shall come from your body, and I will establish his kingdom. He shall build a house for my name, and I will establish the throne of his kingdom forever" (2 Sam. 7:12–13). David, like Paul, realized that the Lord was ultimately speaking not of David's physical son Solomon, but of his future descendant, who would be both son of David and Son of God, namely, the Lord Jesus Christ.

David's son Solomon did build God's temple in Jerusalem, and when the ark of the covenant was brought within its walls, the glory of the Lord filled the place: "A cloud filled the house of the LORD, so that the priests could not stand to minister because of the cloud, for the glory of the LORD filled the house of the LORD" (1 Kings 8:10–11). All of this was symbolic of the true and spiritual fulfillment that would come through Jesus Christ. The true temple is the spiritual house that is Christ's church, which even now is "being joined together . . . into a holy temple in the Lord" (Eph. 2:21). Just as the glory cloud filled Solomon's temple, God wants to fill your life and his church with the Holy Spirit. This is true and saving Christianity, to have God's Spirit live in you, and change you to be holy as a fitting dwelling place for God.

This comparison with the Jewish temple tells us a number of things about the Christian church and about Christian people. The first is that we are saved and the church exists for the sake of God's glory. This is what made the temple in Jerusalem special, that God's presence filled the place with glory.

This leads me to ask, What is it that impresses us about a church or a person? Is it the worldly glory that so attracts the natural man? God's glory is displayed not by sheer numbers or by wealth or by fleshly excitement, but by a people who reverence his Word, who worship in spirit and in truth, who display the fruits of God's Spirit, who adorn their lives with good works, and who wave Christ's banner of love.

The prophet Zechariah spoke about this to an earlier generation of God's people. He was one of the remnant that returned to Jerusalem from the Babylonian exile, to find the temple and the city in ruins. Zechariah's prophecy records a number of visions God gave him, and one of them depicts a man with a measuring line. He was marking out the rebuilding plans according to human wisdom and human reckoning, when an angel was sent to stop him: "Run, say to that young man, 'Jerusalem shall be inhabited as villages without walls, because of the multitude of people and livestock in it. And I will be to her a wall of fire all around, declares the LORD, and I will be the glory in her midst'" (Zech. 2:4–5).

Zechariah's point was the same one that we need to hear today: Do not go about building in a worldly way, according to mere human logic. God promised that he would be his church's strength and that his presence would be her glory: "I will be to her a wall of fire . . . , and I will be [her] glory." Thomas V. Moore comments:

> We learn here the true glory of the Church. It is not in any external pomp or power, of any kind; not in frowning battlements, either of temporal or spiritual pretensions; not in rites and ceremonies, however moss-grown and venerable; not in splendid cathedrals and gorgeous vestments, and the swell of music, and the glitter of eloquence, but in the indwelling glory of the invisible God.[1]

This applies to us as individuals as well as to the church. As the prophet Jeremiah sums up: "Let not the wise man boast in his wisdom, let not the mighty man boast in his might, let not the rich man boast in his riches, but let him who boasts boast in this, that he understands and knows me, that I am the LORD" (Jer. 9:23–24).

The church is, first, for the display of God's glory and, second, holy. The temple was a holy building, that is, it was set apart for the worship of God. Inside were holy vessels, used only for God's service, and holy people, the priests, who were set apart to worship God and serve his people. In the same way, the church is to be set apart. We are not to be worldly. There is to be a noticeable difference between us and the world. This, of course, pertains to sin; as individuals and as a church, we are to be marked by a freedom from sin and by obedience to God's Word. But it goes beyond that, to an active desire to know God and live for him.

This will be reflected in our attitude and our methods of ministry. A generation ago, A. W. Tozer spoke words that have been sadly unheeded by most evangelical churches: "One of the most popular current errors, and the one out of which springs most of the noisy, blustering religious activity in evangelical circles, is the notion that as times change the church must change with them. That mentality which mistakes Hollywood for the Holy City is . . . gravely astray."[2] This is what the apostle John warned the early Christians: "All that is in the world—the desires of the flesh and the desires of the eyes and pride in possessions—is not from the Father but is from the world" (1 John 2:16). In the place of things that impress the flesh and the world, ours is to be a spiritual and holy beauty, one that flows from God's Word as the Spirit uses it to change our lives.

The third thing is that the church, being God's temple, is to be dedicated to the service and worship of God. Paul explains what this means for Christians in Romans 12:1–2: "Present your bodies as a living sacrifice, holy and acceptable to God, which is your spiritual worship. Do not be conformed to this world, but be transformed by the renewal of your mind, that by testing you may discern what is the will of God, what is good and acceptable and perfect."

Whenever you talk about living for God's glory, about being holy, and about serving God with your life, people begin to think dreary thoughts about Christianity and the church. But I want to ask: Is anything more exciting than this? Is anything more wonderful than to realize that my life amounts to more than just occupying space and time, than just getting by and trying to have a decent time? I was made to bear God's image, and in Christ I have been born again so that God himself might live in me and shine forth from me. After everything in this world is gone, I will still be a member of this church that is God's living temple, of which the book of Revelation proclaims, "It shone with the glory of God, and its brilliance was like that of a very precious jewel, like a jasper, clear as crystal. . . . The city does not need the sun or the moon to shine on it, for the glory of God gives it light, and the Lamb is its lamp" (Rev. 21:11, 23 NIV). Realizing this makes me excited about what it means to be a Christian, what it means to be part of Christ's glorious church, the building of which is the greatest project in all eternity.

A Firm Foundation

In introducing his teaching on the church, Paul directs our attention to the all-important matter of the church's foundation. When erecting a building, nothing is more important than laying a solid and true foundation. Paul therefore says that the church is "built on the foundation of the apostles and prophets, Christ Jesus himself being the cornerstone" (Eph. 2:20).

For one thing, if the foundation is the prophets and apostles, then that foundation is laid only once. You do not build by laying a foundation over and over. You build one foundation and then build upward from it.

We sometimes hear today of new apostles. But biblically this is impossible. The apostles were the earthly disciples of Jesus, who bore his own authority in the world and were direct agents of his revelation. By definition, there can be no apostles today, both because no one can fulfill these requirements and because a builder lays a foundation only once. The Roman Catholic Church claims that the pope sits in Peter's office, with his apostolic authority, giving him the right to interpret and even contradict Scripture. But that is impossible, because the apostles' task was to lay the foundation; we now are building up on that foundation, and the apostles' work cannot and need not be repeated.

What did the apostles do in building the church's foundation? In part, they built the foundation by founding the first churches in accordance with God's will. But most significantly, the apostles wrote down for us the completed revelation of God's Word in the New Testament. As one hymn puts it, "How firm a foundation, you saints of the Lord, is laid for your faith in his excellent Word!"[3]

Paul speaks of "the foundation of the apostles and prophets." There is some question whether this refers to the Old Testament prophets. I think this is not likely because in the Greek text these two are grouped together with only one definite article and also because Paul lists the apostles before the prophets, whereas the Old Testament prophets came before the apostles. Paul is probably referring to people who possessed the gift of prophecy spoken of in 1 Corinthians 12 and 14. We need to remember that during the first decades of the church, the New Testament was just being written, and it was many years before the various books were collected and disseminated. The early churches received God's Word through the apostles, but when the apostles moved on, God used prophets to continue giving his Word. Charismatic churches today believe that the gift of prophecy still exists in the church, but Paul tells us here that like the apostles, the New Testament prophets belonged to the foundation-laying apostolic age.

Once the Bible was completed, their function, like that of the apostles, was no longer needed.

What this means for us today is that our foundation as a church must be the apostolic teaching in the Bible. This does not restrict us to the New Testament, since the apostles based their own preaching on the Old Testament. Of the almost eight thousand verses in the New Testament, it is estimated that more than twenty-five hundred quote or refer to the Old Testament.[4] The whole Bible must be the basis for all that we do. Just as a foundation bears the weight of a building and sets the pattern for its growth, so the Bible is the foundation for Christ's church. If we are to build safely, strongly, and faithfully, then we must make God's Word the only infallible rule for our faith and practice. The book of Acts tells us that the church in its earliest days was "devoted . . . to the apostles' teaching" (Acts 2:42), and so must we be today if we are to build on their foundation.

Christ Jesus the Cornerstone

A building is not made secure by just the foundation, but every foundation requires and relies on a cornerstone. In the building of great stone structures, the first thing to be done is to place the cornerstone, on which everything else rests and depends. In God's living temple that is the church, this cornerstone is none other than, Paul says, "Christ Jesus himself" (Eph. 2:20). As the famous hymn puts it: "The church's one foundation is Jesus Christ, her Lord; / she is his new creation by water and the Word: / from heav'n he came and sought her to be his holy bride; / with his own blood he bought her, and for her life he died."[5]

Ephesians 2:20–22 tells us much about Jesus as the cornerstone of the church and corresponds perfectly with everything Paul has previously taught in Ephesians 2. The church consists of those people redeemed and purchased by Jesus with his own precious blood. Ephesians 2:13 says that we who were far away were "brought near by the blood of Christ."

Jesus also created the church through the power of his resurrection. He has created "in himself one new man," verse 15 points out, in the place of all the divisions of the world and by the power of his Holy Spirit. Finally, Christ is the cornerstone because he is Lord over the church. Ephesians 1:22–23 tells us that God "gave him as head over all things to the church, which is his body."

This informs us about the relationship between Christ and the apostles. They are the foundation, and he is the cornerstone. We sometimes hear today that we don't really know what Jesus himself taught, since we have only the version provided to us by the apostles. But that view is in direct contradiction to the Bible's teaching. On the night of his arrest, Jesus told the disciples that his Spirit would come and "guide you into all the truth. . . . He will take what is mine and declare it to you" (John 16:13–14). Before ascending into glory, Jesus breathed the Spirit upon them and said, "You will be my witnesses" (Acts 1:8). Paul was commissioned as an apostle by Jesus himself on the Damascus road. Jesus said to him, "I have appeared to you for this purpose, to appoint you as a servant and witness" (Acts 26:16).

Just as the foundation is the extension of the cornerstone, following its lines and anchored by its strength, so the apostles were Christ's own extension into the world. The apostles and their teaching derive their authority from Jesus himself, and we are to treat their words in the Bible as his own Word to us. In a lesser way, the same is true of us today, and especially of those set apart to the ministry of God's Word. We are to follow Christ's example, we are to serve Christ by the Spirit that he sends, and we are to make God's Word our source of spiritual authority and the only one we need.

The Church Door

According to Paul, Jesus Christ is in the building business. Speaking of the gospel, Jesus promised Peter, "On this rock I will build my church" (Matt. 16:18). Like a magnificent cathedral, Christ's church continues to be built, not one brick but one believer at a time.

And as the billboard says, Jesus starts by buying ugly houses. But he does not just patch them up and sell them. He fills them with glory by his own Spirit. He works a new creation. It begins in our rebirth and continues all through our lives. We are being spiritually renovated with divine power. Jesus gives us a new heart, renews our minds, and fills our souls with the light of God. He is the master builder, and he is himself the cornerstone.

But there is one more thing about Jesus and the church. He is also its door. Jesus is the only way you can enter this spiritual house, the only way you can be built into this living temple that is filled with the glory of God. Jesus said, "I am the door. If anyone enters by me, he will be saved" (John 10:9).

This is illustrated by the story of a young woman who came to church with a friend and soon realized that there was something seriously different about it. People talked about having a personal relationship with Jesus Christ. Someone asked her a jarring question: "If you were to die tonight and stand before God, and if he were to ask you, 'Why should I let you into my heaven?' what would you say?" She answered that she had received the sacraments and that though not perfect she was a basically good person. She then was invited to ask the question back, and the Christian answered in a very different way. He said his only hope was that Jesus Christ had died on the cross for his sins. When the conversation was over, she turned to her friend and said, "Wow, those answers were completely different!" The church's pastor later remembered:

"Even though she was not yet a Christian, she could see that there was an eternity of difference between asking God to accept her on her own merits and asking him to let what Jesus did count for her. Not long afterwards the Holy Spirit brought her to saving faith in Jesus Christ."[6]

This is the key point for anyone who is not part of God's great and spiritual house, who is not God's child, and who does not know what it means to be a citizen in God's kingdom. The only way you can be saved from your sins and enter into the blessings of God is through faith in Jesus Christ. He is the door, and if you will believe in him, you will be saved. Then you will become a part of his glorious church, the temple he is building for the dwelling of God forever.

But let me complete the woman's story for the sake of those who already believe. Sometime later, the woman reflected on what had happened and lamented that in all the years she had attended church, no one had ever given her the gospel. No one had explained the cross and the free gift of Christ's imputed righteousness through faith alone. She had thought it was just up to her to be good enough for God. Do you see why it is important that we build the church in the right way—on the gospel foundation of the apostles and on the cornerstone that is Christ, with Jesus himself as the door? Jesus said, "If anyone enters by me, he will be saved" (John 10:9). If we bring people into the church through any door other than Christ himself, then we do not bring them to salvation. They may be happy here, they may have felt needs met, but they will not be saved. We can bring people in through all sorts of different doors, literally and figuratively. But they will be saved and be a part of God's spiritual house only if they enter through Christ, only if they trust in his life, death, and resurrection for their salvation.

I praise the Lord that that woman could come to a church near her, a church to which a caring Christian invited her, and a church where the gospel was not only preached from the pulpit but shared by a whole church of living witnesses. That is the kind of church that God is calling us to be, and if we are faithful to our Lord, we are promised that by the Spirit he will build us up together "into a holy temple in the Lord . . . into a dwelling place for God by the Spirit."

Questions for Study and Reflection

1. What does the author mean by suggesting that Jesus "buys ugly houses"?
2. How are the Jewish temple of the Old Testament and the Christian church of the New Testament historically linked? If the church fulfills God's intention through the temple, what sorts of thoughts does this provoke regarding the church? What is the true glory and the true strength of the church?
3. How are the apostles the "foundation" of the church? Discuss the author's argument regarding the possibility of apostles today or the doctrine of "apostolic succession." Does any of this make a real difference?
4. What does a cornerstone do? Why is it so important to a building? How does Jesus Christ function as the cornerstone for his church? And once we realize this, how should it inform our approach to worship and ministry in the church today?
5. How does Jesus function as the church door? Is it possible for a church to be biblically faithful and also culturally effective? What are your thoughts about this?

Notes

Preface

1. D. Martyn Lloyd-Jones, *God's Way of Reconciliation: An Exposition of Ephesians 2* (Grand Rapids: Baker, 1972), vii.

Chapter 1: Dead in Sin

1. Klyne Snodgrass, *Ephesians* (Grand Rapids: Zondervan, 1996), 93.
2. Harold S. Kushner, *How Good Do We Have to Be?* (Boston: Little, Brown and Company, 1996), 30–31.
3. D. Martyn Lloyd-Jones, *God's Way of Reconciliation: An Exposition of Ephesians 2* (Grand Rapids: Baker, 1972), 19.
4. R. Kent Hughes, *Ephesians: The Mystery of the Body of Christ* (Wheaton: Crossway, 1990), 66.
5. St. Augustine, *City of God* (repr., New York: Doubleday, 1958), 279.
6. Ibid., 313.
7. John Calvin, *Sermons on Ephesians* (1562; repr., Edinburgh: Banner of Truth, 1993), 37.
8. J. C. Ryle, *Holiness* (1879; repr., Durham, UK: Evangelical Press, 1979), 3.
9. John MacArthur, *Ephesians* (Chicago: Moody, 1986), 52–53.
10. J. I. Packer, *Knowing God* (Downers Grove, IL: InterVarsity, 1973), 136.

Chapter 2: The World, the Devil, and the Flesh

1. D. Martyn Lloyd-Jones, *God's Way of Reconciliation: An Exposition of Ephesians 2* (Grand Rapids: Baker, 1972), 15.
2. Leon Morris, *Expository Reflections on Ephesians* (Grand Rapids: Baker, 1994), 42.
3. D. Martyn Lloyd-Jones, *Expositions on the Sermon on the Mount*, 2 vols. (Grand Rapids: Eerdmans, 1959), 1:37.
4. James Montgomery Boice, *Ephesians* (Grand Rapids: Baker, 1998), 50.

5. Quoted in William Barclay, *The Letters to the Galatians and Ephesians* (Philadelphia: Westminster, 1976), 100.

6. Charles Haddon Spurgeon, in *Spurgeon's Sermons*, 10 vols. (Grand Rapids: Baker, 1883), 5:273.

7. Ibid., 5:274.

8. Ibid., 5:286.

Chapter 3: But God

1. D. Martyn Lloyd-Jones, *God's Way of Reconciliation: An Exposition of Ephesians 2* (Grand Rapids: Baker, 1972), 59.

2. D. Martyn Lloyd-Jones, *God's Way, Not Ours* (Grand Rapids: Baker, 1998), 88.

3. Ibid.

4. Ibid.

5. Augustus M. Toplady, "Rock of Ages, Cleft for Me" (1776), *Trinity Hymnal* (Suwanee, GA: Great Commission Publications, 1990), no. 499, stzs. 2–3.

6. John Owen, *Communion with God*, abridged by R. J. K. Law (repr., Edinburgh: Banner of Truth, 1991), 82–83.

7. Quoted in Bryan Chapell, *The Promises of Grace* (Grand Rapids: Baker, 2001), 136–37.

8. James M. Boice, *Ephesians: An Expositional Commentary* (Grand Rapids: Baker, 1997), 54.

Chapter 4: Spiritual Resurrection

1. D. Martyn Lloyd-Jones, *The Life of Peace: An Exposition of Philippians 3 & 4* (Grand Rapids: Baker, 1990), 49–50.

2. D. Martyn Lloyd-Jones, *God's Way of Reconciliation: An Exposition of Ephesians 2* (Grand Rapids: Baker, 1972), 79.

3. James Montgomery Boice, *Romans*, 4 vols. (Grand Rapids: Baker, 1992), 2:678.

4. John R. W. Stott, *Men Made New: An Exposition of Romans 6–8* (Downers Grove, IL: InterVarsity, 1994), 48–49.

Chapter 5: Together with Christ

1. Hugh Martin, *Christ for Us: Sermons of Hugh Martin* (Edinburgh: Banner of Truth Trust, 1998), 48–66.

2. Ibid., 50.

3. Quoted in James Montgomery Boice, *Ephesians: An Expositional Commentary* (Grand Rapids: Baker, 1998), 59.

4. See the more extensive treatment of our spiritual resurrection in the previous chapter.

5. Chris Palmer, "Reinventing the Wheel," *ESPN The Magazine* (July 28, 2008): 52–58.

6. D. Martyn Lloyd-Jones, *God's Way of Reconciliation: An Exposition of Ephesians 2* (Grand Rapids: Baker, 1972), 89.

7. C. Austin Miles, "In the Garden" (1912), *The Service Hymnal* (Chicago: Hope Publishing, 1946), no. 445.

8. William Barclay, *The Letters to the Galatians and Ephesians* (Philadelphia: Westminster, 1976), 103.

Chapter 6: The Glory of God in Salvation

1. Quoted in Ravi Zacharias, *Can Man Live without God?* (Dallas: Word, 1994), 56.

2. Sinclair B. Ferguson, *Discovering God's Will* (Edinburgh: Banner of Truth, 1982), 16.

3. E. J. Young, *Isaiah,* 3 vols. (Grand Rapids: Eerdmans, 1993), 1:245–46.

4. Hugh Martin, *Christ for Us: Sermons of Hugh Martin* (Edinburgh: Banner of Truth, 1998), 213.

5. Donald Grey Barnhouse, *Expositions of Bible Doctrines Taking the Epistle to the Romans as a Point of Departure,* 10 vols. (Grand Rapids: Eerdmans, 1953, reprint, 1994), 2:165-166.

6. John Owen, *Communion with God* (repr., Edinburgh: Banner of Truth, 1991), 86.

7. D. Martyn Lloyd-Jones, *God's Way of Reconciliation: An Exposition of Ephesians 2* (Grand Rapids: Baker, 1972), 116.

8. James Montgomery Boice, *Romans,* 4 vols. (Grand Rapids: Baker, 1993), 3:1108–9.

Chapter 7: By Grace, through Faith

1. D. Martyn Lloyd-Jones, *Faith Tried and Triumphant* (Grand Rapids: Baker, 1965; reprint, 1987), 171.

2. A. W. Tozer, *The Knowledge of the Holy* (San Francisco: HarperCollins, 1961; reprint, 1992), 145–46.

3. Norman Vincent Peale, *The Power of Positive Thinking* (New York: Prentice-Hall, 1952), 99.

4. Charles Haddon Spurgeon, in *Spurgeon's Sermons,* 10 vols. (Grand Rapids: Baker, 1883), 3:260.

5. Arthur W. Pink, *The Life of David* (Grand Rapids: Baker, 1981), 260–61.

6. Adapted from Leon Morris, *Expository Reflections on the Letter to the Ephesians* (Grand Rapids: Baker, 1994), 104.

7. Augustus Toplady, "Rock of Ages, Cleft for Me" (1776), *Trinity Hymnal* (Suwanee, GA: Great Commission Publications, 1990), no. 499, stz. 2.

Chapter 8: God's Workmanship

1. See, for instance, Zane Hodges, *Absolutely Free: A Biblical Reply to Lordship Salvation* (Grand Rapids: Zondervan, 1989), and Charles Ryrie, *So Great Salvation: What It Means to Believe in Jesus Christ* (Chicago: Moody, 1997).

2. Charles Haddon Spurgeon, in *Spurgeon's Sermons,* 10 vols. (Grand Rapids: Baker, 1883), 1:81.

3. G. Campbell Morgan, *The Westminster Pulpit,* 10 vols. (Grand Rapids: Baker, 1995), 1:245.

4. Adapted from R. Kent Hughes, *Ephesians: The Mystery of the Body of Christ* (Wheaton: Crossway, 1990), 82–83.

5. D. Martyn Lloyd-Jones, *God's Way of Reconciliation: An Exposition of Ephesians 2* (Grand Rapids: Baker, 1972), 151.

Chapter 9: Without Christ

1. William Barclay, *The Letters to the Galatians and Ephesians* (Philadelphia: Westminster, 1976), 107.

2. Ibid.

3. D. Martyn Lloyd-Jones, *God's Way of Reconciliation: An Exposition of Ephesians 2* (Grand Rapids: Baker, 1972), 169.

4. Geoffrey B. Wilson, *Ephesians* (Edinburgh: Banner of Truth, 1978), 53.

5. Lloyd-Jones, *God's Way of Reconciliation,* 170.

6. Neil Postman, *Amusing Ourselves to Death: Public Discourse in the Age of Show Business* (New York: Penguin, 1986).

7. Quoted in Ravi Zacharias, *Can Man Live without God?* (Dallas: Word, 1994), 58.

8. Ibid., 51.

9. Theognis, quoted in Barclay, *Galatians and Ephesians,* 110.

10. Quoted in James Montgomery Boice and Philip Graham Ryken, *The Heart of the Cross* (Wheaton, IL: Crossway, 1999), 13.

11. Quoted in J. C. Ryle, *Light from Old Times* (Moscow, ID: Charles Nolan, 1890; reprint, 2000), 134.

12. Quoted in Zacharias, *Can Man Live without God?* 56.

13. Charles Haddon Spurgeon, *Metropolitan Tabernacle Pulpit,* 63 vols. (Pasadena, TX: Pilgrim Publications, 1980), 61:366.

Chapter 10: Brought Near to God

1. D. Martyn Lloyd-Jones, *God's Way of Reconciliation: An Exposition of Ephesians 2* (Grand Rapids: Baker, 1972), 187.

2. H. Maldwyn Hughes, quoted in James Montgomery Boice and Philip Graham Ryken, *The Heart of the Cross* (Wheaton, IL: Crossway, 1999), 148.

Chapter 11: Christ, Our Peace

1. Tacitus, *Agricola*, 30.

2. James Montgomery Boice, *Ephesians* (Grand Rapids: Baker, 1998), 85.

3. James Montgomery Boice and Philip Graham Ryken, *The Heart of the Cross* (Wheaton, IL: Crossway, 1999), 148.

4. John Calvin, *Calvin's New Testament Commentaries*, 12 vols., T.H.L. Parker, trans. (Grand Rapids: Eerdmans, 1965), 11:150.

Chapter 12: The New Humanity

1. This is referred to as the *homogeneous unit principle.*

Chapter 13: Access to the Father

1. D. Martyn Lloyd-Jones, *The Kingdom of God* (Wheaton, IL: Crossway, 1992), 82.

2. Philip Graham Ryken, *The Prayer of Our Lord* (Wheaton, IL: Crossway, 2002), 21–22.

3. Lloyd-Jones, *The Kingdom of God*, 82.

Chapter 14: Citizens and Children

1. William Edgar, "Disillusioned," in *Finding God at Harvard*, ed. Kelly Monroe (Grand Rapids: Zondervan, 1996), 62.

2. James Montgomery Boice, *Ephesians* (Grand Rapids: Baker, 1998), 90.

3. D. Martyn Lloyd-Jones, *God's Way of Reconciliation* (Grand Rapids: Baker, 1972), 328.

4. Hattie E. Buell, "A Child of the King" (1877), *Trinity Hymnal* (Suwanee, GA: Great Commission Publications, 1990), no. 525, stz. 3.

5. William Edgar, *Reasons of the Heart* (Grand Rapids: Baker, 1996), 59.

6. Ibid.

Chapter 15: A Holy Temple

1. T. V. Moore, *Haggai, Zechariah and Malachi* (Edinburgh: Banner of Truth, 1979), 141.

2. A. W. Tozer, *Renewed Day by Day: A Daily Devotional* (Camp Hill, PA: Christian Publications, 1980), Feb. 7.

3. "How Firm a Foundation" (1787), *Trinity Hymnal* (Suwanee, GA: Great Commission Publications, 1990), no. 94, stz. 1.

4. Richard D. Phillips, Philip G. Ryken, and Mark E. Dever, *The Church: One, Holy, Catholic, and Apostolic* (Phillipsburg, NJ: P&R Publishing, 2004), 104.

5. Samuel J. Stone, "The Church's One Foundation" (1866), *Trinity Hymnal,* no. 347, stz. 1.

6. Phillips, Ryken, and Dever, *The Church,* 114–15.

Index of Scripture

Index of Subjects and Names

Richard D. Phillips (M.Div. Westminster Theological Seminary) is senior minister of the historic Second Presbyterian Church in Greenville, South Carolina. The author of numerous books on the Bible, theology, and Christian living, including commentaries on Hebrews, Zechariah, and a forthcoming commentary on Jonah–Micah, he is also series coeditor of the Reformed Expository Commentary. A member of the councils of the Gospel Coalition and the Alliance of Confessing Evangelicals, Phillips is chairman of the Philadelphia Conference on Reformed Theology, and his radio preaching ministry, *God's Living Word,* is heard on stations throughout America. He lives in the upcountry of South Carolina with his wife and five children.